STAR TREK
DISCOVERY

GUIDE TO SEASONS 1 AND 2
COLLECTOR'S EDITION

CONTENTS

DISCOVER THE NEXT ADVENTURE

In 2017, after an absence of a dozen years, *Star Trek* warped back onto the small screen, in the form of *Star Trek: Discovery*. Though set 10 years prior to the original series, this was nevertheless a radical, fresh take on *Trek*, with a brand new cast, a gleaming new ship, and a decidedly contemporary approach to storytelling.

This special collection of articles and interviews traces the development of the show, from launch, though to the first season, into the second season, and beyond...

"EVERY SINGLE EPISODE DELVES SO DEEPLY INTO RELATIONSHIPS, INTO EMOTION, AND INTO WHAT IT REALLY MEANS TO BE ALIVE."

Sonequa Martin-Green, First Officer Michael Burnham

The intricate Klingon Torchbearer costume at the *Star Trek Discovery* gallery exhibition

STAR TREK
DISCOVERY

LAUNCHING DISCOVERY

San Diego International Comic-Con 2017 saw the promotional trail for *Star Trek: Discovery* get fully underway, as the series made its bid to wrest public attention away from countless superhero flicks and retail opportunities.

Star Trek Magazine was given special access to the cast and producers of the new series during the convention, and we took the opportunity to dig a little deeper into how this *Trek* – and its core cast of characters– will bring something new to the 50-year-old franchise.

Words: Tara Bennett

Captain Georgiou (Michelle Yeoh) and first officer Michael Burnham (Sonequa Martin-Green)

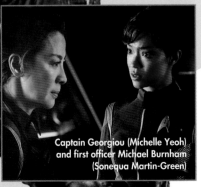

Jason Isaacs as Captain Gabriel Lorca

Over the past 47 years, San Diego Comic-Con International has grown into the world's premier pop culture event. Every July, more than 200,000 comic, movie and TV fans gather to be wowed by brand new theatrical trailers, themed activities, celebrity-filled panels, and an entire convention floor jammed with incredible things to buy. For any new film or television show to drop the mic at the event, leaving behind a flurry of excitement and buzz, means that property did it right.

It's no surprise then that *Star Trek: Discovery* was one of the big hitters at SDCC 2017, debuting a stunning cinematic trailer and introducing key members of the cast for fans to meet and greet. The CBS production also showed off its Starfleet uniforms, Klingon wardrobe and armaments, phasers, and concept art in a visually stunning gallery exhibition.

The excitement in the air was palpable, and Trekkers – who have waited patiently for new television *Trek* for over a decade – seemed more than happy with what they got to see.

Star Trek: Discovery's executive producer Alex Kurtzman, for one, is excited that they are excited. Speaking to *STM* after the main SDCC panel, he was confident that the new series would appeal to long-term fans by adhering to what made the original so great, but with a modern twist. He puts this down to the platforms that *Star Trek: Discovery* will air on (CBS All Access, and internationally on Netflix), which have enabled the writers to fully embrace modern, serialized storytelling.

"To be able to approach this as one long story, as opposed to a more close-ended approach, is liberating beyond belief," Kurtzman enthused. "It actually allows us to do *Trek* in a new way. We have to preserve and protect all the ideals of *Trek*, but from a storytelling point of view it's so much more interesting, both as a writer and for me as an audience member, to watch something that is unresolved at the end of every week. That carries an emotional through line where characters grow and learn over the course of a season. From that point of view, it couldn't be more exciting."

Alex Kurtzman, Sonequa Martin-Green, Jason Isaacs, and Doug Jones at SDCC

Rainn Wilson plays a younger, more dastardly Harry Mudd in *Discovery*

"THIS IS A DARKER TIME IN *STAR TREK: DISCOVERY*. THEY'RE AT WAR, SO IT'S A DARKER, EDGIER HARRY MUDD."

Rainn Wilson, Harry Mudd

"The sets are larger than people imagine," he told us with genuine awe. "More of the show is actually shot practically. A lot of what we're seeing these days, a lot of big science fiction movies and television shows, have a tremendous amount of digital set extension. But our sets are for real. I've rarely seen sets this big, this articulated, this complex, and this staggering. What happens then is that the action can be very organic, as if they're really occupying the ship. I think it's unprecedented. I've never seen *Star Trek* sets as practically executed."

Kurtzman agreed, adding, "We have the biggest stages in Toronto. They're just massive stages, and they're incredibly high, so you get a sense of the world not just in the depth of it, but in the height of it. There's no set extension. Really the only thing you're getting that's CG is the space in the background."

THE *TREK* LOOK

Although set a decade before the original series, *Discovery* is obviously being produced over half a century later, and consequently benefits from advances in production techniques that Gene Roddenberry's creative staff could only have dreamed of. That's reflected in the updated designs of classic *Star Trek* props, like the phaser and communicator on display at a special gallery exhibition not far from the main Comic-Con site. It's clear *Discovery* references the past, but strives for a look of its own.

When we spoke to executive producer Akiva Goldsman about the visuals aspect of the series, he confirmed that, contrary to what many might expect, *Star Trek: Discovery* is very practical in terms of its vision of the future.

NUMBER ONE

Populating these vast sets are a group of actors led by ex-*Walking Dead* star Sonequa Martin-Green, who plays *U.S.S. Shenzhou* First Officer Michael Burnham. Martin-Green's character is a human who was raised as a Vulcan by astrophysicist Sarek (James Frain). She describes Burnham as "a woman of principle. She's a woman of duty. She's a woman of culture. She values culture, and understanding everyone and everything that she comes into contact with."

It's not lost on the actress that Burnham is just one position away from the Captain's chair, which is a big deal for a woman of color in this particular TV universe.

"I think it's important, because people need to see themselves," the actress asserted with passion. "That's what storytelling should be. It

Burnham's Starfleet issue space suit

Cast and producers arrive at the *Discovery* gallery exhibition by *Trek*-themed rickshaw (Left to right: Anthony Rapp, Akiva Goldsman, Mary Wiseman, Jason Isaacs, Doug Jones, Sonequa Martin-Green, James Frain, Aaron Harberts and Gretchen J. Berg)

Martin-Green greets fans outside the *Discovery* gallery

Inside, fans were able to get up close to props and costumes which had been in use on set just days before

should be a mirror to society. Unfortunately, we've had so many stories told in TV and in film that aren't true mirrors to what we really look like in our world today. I think that people can only understand their full potential when they see what they can do. That's why the entertainment industry and theater, and all of these stories, shape us so deeply, because we see what can be. That's why it's so important to see every bit of diversity that we have so people can see themselves, and then they can aspire to be something greater."

Martin-Green is also incredibly happy that the *Discovery* scripts are filled with important themes, telling stories that question what our potential can be, in the most *Star Trek* of ways.

"Every single episode delves so deeply into relationships, into emotion, and into what it really means to be alive, regardless of what being you may be," said Martin-Green. "That's what's

going to bring us together in this new *Star Trek* community, and keep us coming back to each other. Keeping us passionate as we tell this story. Keeping you passionate as you see it. Because every single episode goes courageously into the hearts of the people and the aliens, and we haven't seen that done before in the way that we're doing it."

CREWMATES

Given what we saw in the trailer released at Comic-Con, the fate of the *Shenzhou* and its crew looks uncertain, but luckily crewmates from the *U.S.S. Discovery*'s engineering division made it to San Diego, and shared further details on how their characters play into the broader tapestry.

Mary Wiseman, who plays Cadet Sylvia Tilly, told us that Tilly is "super un-confident when we first meet her. She's isolated and very, very nervous, and feels very small. Through exposure

to all these wonderful characters, I think she's starting to come into herself and figure out how she can be a functioning, helpful, and important member of the ship."

Science Officer Lt. Paul Stamets works alongside Tilly in engineering, and actor Anthony Rapp admitted that his character isn't exactly the easiest crewman to get along with on the ship.

"He's incredibly smart, and when you're that smart, sometimes it's hard to be around other people who aren't as smart about some things," the actor said with a smile. "It's been very interesting to see how that plays out. He's not the most adept at interpersonal relationships, so it's been really interesting to see the way that that's evolved and changed over the course of the season."

Following the lead set by the *Kelvin* timeline's Hikaru Sulu in *Star Trek Beyond*,

Concept art on display at the *Discovery* gallery

Cast members grab a few selfies during the *Discovery* panel at SDCC

Stamets will be *Star Trek*'s first homosexual character to have an ongoing relationship threaded into the storyline of the series. As *Discovery* begins, Stamet's will already be in a long-term partnership with Chief Medical Officer Hugh Culber, played by Wilson Cruz.

"One of the things we establish is that my partner totally gets me. He gets that aspect of me that can be a little bit off-putting," Rapp said of their relationship. "[Hugh] has opened his arms and heart up to Stamets in a wonderful way."

Rapp added that he's impressed with *Star Trek: Discovery*'s writers, and how they don't shine a light on that relationship any differently to others on the ship.

"I'm on the bridge, and you haven't met all of the junior bridge officers yet. It's a panoply of every kind of person, but there's nothing in the text at all about it. It speaks to a Utopian vision,

what is to come, where hopefully none of those differences matter. I'm thrilled to be a part of something that looks like that."

Another character stationed aboard *Discovery* has a very different story to tell, and looks to carry some baggage when we first encounter him. Shazad Latif, originally cast as a Klingon, plays the intense Lieutenant Ash Tyler, a former prisoner of war who has been damaged by his experiences.

"He's gone through these horrible, horrible things," Latif explained. "We explore that, and he explores that with other people in the ship."

Tyler forms a special relationship with Captain Lorca (Jason Isaacs), who helps Tyler in his transition back into service.

"There's a military connection there. There's a bond there," added Latif, before teasing: "And then there's a chemistry, a relationship with Burnham that he's exploring."

MUDD STICKS

Two of the most-anticipated roles on *Star Trek: Discovery* are the younger versions of Spock's Vulcan father, Sarek, who is played by James Frain, and intergalactic troublemaker Harcourt Fenton Mudd, played by ex-*The Office* star Rainn Wilson.

Burnham (Martin-Green) in action, in a scene from the *Discovery* trailer that thrilled fans at San Diego Comic-Con

From the original series through to *The Next Generation*, Sarek was portrayed with a gentle nobility by actor Mark Lenard. In *Discovery*, renowned British actor James Frain slips into the Vulcan robes, and he admitted that it has been a fascinating journey already.

"I haven't had quite this experience before. Usually you have some sense of the whole journey of the character and who the character is, but I'm literally exploring it as we go along, and finding the different colors."

Frain conceded that it's been challenging to play a character intentionally devoid of emotion.

"It's really demanding to have your emotional life so completely in check," Frain laughed. "Sometimes I feel like I'm not doing much, but they're like, 'No. You're fine. You're not moving an inch.' I'm like, 'Okay. Good. That should do it.'

"TO BE ABLE TO APPROACH THIS AS ONE LONG STORY, AS OPPOSED TO A MORE CLOSE-ENDED APPROACH, IS LIBERATING BEYOND BELIEF."
Alex Kurtzman, Executive Producer

"It's really interesting, the Vulcan ideal where they came to the conclusion that emotion, all emotion, is a problem," he continued. "That is so alien to us. Ultimately, is it really achievable? And who is this alien guy that marries a human being? I mean, how did that happen? Answering that is what I feel like I'm doing every day."

Actor Rainn Wilson, meanwhile, is giddy to make the transition from life-long *Star Trek* fan to playing one of the original series' very few recurring characters, and a much-loved one at that.

"It's almost Shakespearean, with his heightened language," Wilson said of Mudd, obviously thrilled at winning the part. "And to get to play a civilian is rare in *Star Trek*. There's this whole universe where they're buying things, and selling things, and trading things, and having cities, and falling in love. We need to see some of those characters sometimes."

Mudd is a recurring role that Wilson confirmed will appear in two episodes.

"But they're pretty meaty episodes," Wilson stressed. "He gets a lot to do. They really, really went for it with Harry Mudd. I was a huge fan of the original series, and they had some straight-up comedy episodes, which is great. You've got to mix it up when you're doing 22 episodes a year, and that was part of the Roddenberry universe. But this is a darker time in *Star Trek: Discovery*. They're at war, so it's a darker, edgier Harry Mudd."

Originally played by Roger C. Carmel, Wilson says he had no qualms about stepping into such a sacred character's shoes. "Let me put it this way. I inherited the role of Dwight [Schrute from *The Office*] from Mackenzie Crook in the original UK series. I basically stole all of the brilliant stuff that he did, and then added my own stuff, and it was great," Wilson smiled. "It's the same thing with this. I inherited a character that had been previously played by another brilliant actor. I stole a lot of things that I loved from his performance, and then added a lot more of my own. It's a testament to Roger C. Carmel, to what an interesting actor he was. You can't take your eyes off him when he's in an episode. So full of light. The new writers have added that he's mischievous and deadly at the same time, and that's a fun balance to watch."

Wilson's self-effacing summation of what he brings to Mudd could also sum up what the creators of *Star Trek: Discovery* have done with the series that we've known and loved for generations – they've taken all the "brilliant stuff" that Gene Roddenberry and so many others created, and added something of their own, something of the now. And *Star Trek* lives! ▲

SONEQUA MARTIN-GREEN INTERVIEW

HUMAN BORN
VULCAN BRED

Star Trek's new leading lady, Sonequa Martin-Green, has walked away from *The Walking Dead* and boldly toward the final frontier. Now, *Discovery*'s Michael Burnham can finally reveal how *Star Trek* gave her a Buzz Lightyear moment.

Words: Bryan Cairns

onequa Martin-Green knows she's on the cusp of making history with *CBS All Access'* highly anticipated *Trek* revival, *Star Trek: Discovery.* Back in 1966, Gene Roddenberry's original *Star Trek* series championed diversity and equality through its storytelling and casting. African-American Nichelle Nichols monitored communications as Lt. Uhura; soft-spoken Sulu, portrayed by Asian-American George Takei, helmed the *U.S.S. Enterprise*; and the following year, Russian Walter Koenig joined the cast as navigator Pavel Chekov.

Discovery continues to honor that tradition of breaking new ground by featuring the first female black lead of the franchise, Martin-Green's Michael Burnham. The gravity, responsibility,

and impact of such an unprecedented, progressive move was not lost on the actor.

"It says the sky is the limit for all of us," Sonequa told *Star Trek Magazine* during a tour of the *Discovery* sets in Toronto. "What we're seeing now in our media is this push to diminish, and to devalue, and to make people feel the sky is not the limit for them, and that they are meant for the ground. Having me as the first black lead of a *Star Trek* series just blasts that into a million pieces.

"That's what we need right now. I think we need to turn to each other," she continues. "We need to turn to good storytelling, and we need to turn to art. We need to turn to these things to see the solution. This show serves as that. I am eternally grateful that we are now

part of the conversation, and hopefully a part of, as cliché as it sounds, making the world a better place, because I really believe it. I think it's vital."

Best known as Sasha on the popular zombie drama series *The Walking Dead*, Martin-Green's other credits include *The Good Wife*, *NYC 22*, and *Once Upon a Time*. Ironically, Martin-Green's involvement with *The Walking Dead* nearly prevented her from doing *Discovery* at all. Former showrunner Bryan Fuller approached Martin-Green about joining the space saga, but she still needed to fulfill her zombie apocalypse obligations. As a result, Martin-Green assumed her lack of availability closed the door on anything *Star Trek* related. And then *Discovery*'s premiere date got delayed.

"At that time, such a monumental chapter in my life was closing with *The Walking Dead*," Martin-Green recalls. "I was in such a place of contentment and peace about everything. I was excited for what was next. I was excited to turn the page. I was just trusting what was happening. As I was shooting those last few episodes of my end on *Walking Dead* – and then *Star Trek* came – it felt like a snug fit. It really did, but it moved on for me because of the scheduling conflicts. So, I said, 'You know what? It felt like a snug fit, but, it's gone, so that's fine. I trust what's happening. I trust what's meant to be will be.' I let it go. I just focused on ending my journey on *Walking Dead*, and I gave that my all. Then *Star Trek*

01 Burnham and Captain Georgiou (Michelle Yeoh) prepare to transport.

02 A trek through the desert for Burnham and her captain.

03 First Officer Michael Burnham (Sonequa Martin-Green).

MICHAEL BURNHAM
FIRST OFFICER

When her family was killed by Klingons while under Vulcan jurisdiction, Michael Burnham was taken in and adopted by Sarek, a Vulcan Ambassador, and his human wife, Amanda. They raised the girl as their own, alongside their son, Spock.

Burnham developed a particularly strong bond with Sarek, and became a disciple of the Vulcan philosopher Surak, the father of modern Vulcan culture. She learned how to suppress her destructive, human emotions, and master logic, but sometimes felt she was becoming more Vulcan than human, and she found that realization troubling.

Burnham studied at the Vulcan Science Academy on Vulcan before joining Starfleet, and rose to become first officer on the *U.S.S. Shenzhou*, under the command of Captain Philippa Georgiou. Burnham grew under Georgiou, finding a second mother in her Starfleet captain, until the war with the Klingons set her on a new path.

came around again. I said, 'I knew it was a snug fit.'"

Speaking of Fuller, over the years, he's gained a reputation for bestowing his female protagonists with traditionally male names. Well, he did that here, too, with Michael Burnham.

"What I decided was I was named after my biological father," Martin-Green offers. "What's really beautiful about that is that we explore a father/daughter dynamic on our show, definitely between Sarek [James Frain] and I. You also have this subtle, yet powerful, nod to it as well because we can look to the future where gender roles are more fluid, where a woman can have a male name, and a woman can be named after her father. Or, a son can be named after his mother. It's quite innovative."

To help find Burnham's voice, Martin-Green admits to spending plenty of time watching the original *Star Trek* TV series. In particular, she found Spock's first officer "profound."

"Leonard Nimoy's performance is amazing," Martin-Green says, full of praise. "I love Zachary Quinto's performance as well, but Leonard captured such a charm. He found the humor and the dryness. He found a way to somehow be vulnerable, but completely objective at the same time. It really speaks to his talent. It has to do with why Spock is a popular, favorite character. It has everything to do with Leonard, so I watched him a lot. But, in terms of who I modeled myself after, it's just the story. There's a lot going on, so I just had to dig into all these different facets of who I am, as Michael Burnham, and try to make them as real as I could. I'm still doing that."

Who Am I?

Even though *Discovery* kicked off production at the start of 2017, plot points surrounding the show's direction – and Martin-Green's character – have remained scarce. However, during the *Star Trek: Discovery* panel at 2017's San Diego Comic-Con, certain information emerged. We already knew that *Discovery* takes place 10 years before the original series, and that Burnham serves as first officer on the *U.S.S. Shenzhou*, but the producers chose the occasion to drop the bombshell that Burnham was Spock's adopted sister.

Spock's father, Sarek, raised Burnham from a young age after her parents' demise. As a child, she became the only human to attend the Vulcan Learning Center and, subsequently, Vulcan Science Academy. Martin-Green believes Burnham's unique upbringing

will deliver plenty of narrative opportunities and inner conflict.

"I like the struggle it provides from a storytelling perspective," the actress explains. "It's evocative. It's provocative because we've seen Spock struggle with the dichotomy of his identity, by literally being half-Vulcan and half-human. I am fully human, but I have been indoctrinated with a new culture. Here I am, being Michael Burnham. Now, we have struggles that come from culture shock. I did grow up as a human for a while before my parents were killed, and then was thrown into this Vulcan way of life.

"There was the fight to assimilate what I had to deal with," she says of Burnham's personal struggles. "That's trauma, all on its own. So, I take all of that – I take the identity crisis of that right into Starfleet – and then how I operate, as the first officer,

> ## "As I was shooting those last few episodes of my end on *Walking Dead* – and then *Star Trek* came – it felt like a snug fit. It really did."
>
> SONEQUA MARTIN-GREEN

whether I lean into my Vulcan logic or I lean toward my human emotion, these are things I have to ask myself daily.

"But it's not so binary, where it's just Vulcan or human," Martin-Green continues. "It's a lot more multi-layered than that. There are all these principles swimming around in my mind and my heart. I have to decide, 'Who am I? Who am I going to be?' I think anybody that has to deal with acculturation has to ask that question. Anybody who moves away from home, once they've come of age, they have to ask themselves, 'Am I going to be that person or a new person?' This is all part of the *Discovery*."

Martin-Green reveled in contemplating Burnham and Spock's childhood together. After all, that was uncharted territory, since Spock had never mentioned her existence.

"Spock is my favorite person in the canon," Martin-Green enthuses. "I know he's a lot of people's favorite. Spock is an institution in the canon, as is Sarek.

Now, of course, I look at him differently. I'm constantly building and creating, so I see him now and go, 'Oh… Spock. I see you running around the house. I see you walking around the house in a very weird way.' It's been fun building memories with him involved."

Star Trek and its spin-offs commenced with the main crew and their mission established, with the occasional fine-tuning here and there. However, the captains – Kirk, Picard, Sisko, Janeway, and Archer – were all firmly in place. *Discovery* plans to zero in on an ambitious first officer, who wants to eventually take command and literally sit in the driver's seat. Burnham's exchanges with fellow crewmembers, and her wrestling with the crisis at hand, this Federation/Klingon war, will shape her over the season.

"It's very courageous," notes Martin-Green about shifting focus from a captain to a first officer. "It was a brave decision for them to do that. It offers more avenues of storytelling. You are able to see more. You are able to experience more, because I'm experiencing more. I'm not this permanent fixture who has

04

05

grown into who I am, where it's already been done, and I've been defined, I know who I am, what I've done, and I'm already here. I think there's a place for that, but when you can instead go on the journey with me of self-discovery – of my journey to captain – you can see how that happens.

"That's something we've never seen happen before," she says. "It would be wildly interesting to see any of the captains that we know from the *Star Trek* canon go from first officer to captain. What was Captain Kirk's journey like? It offers a tremendous opportunity to engage, because you see an aspirational path we've never seen before.

"When you can see people actually change – whether that be for good or for bad – that's one of the most exciting, exhilarating things about serialized storytelling. Seeing how decisions lead to someone's development," Martin-Green adds. "You go on that journey with me, day by day by day, as I'm being changed, and shifting my decisions by the people that I'm interacting with, by the people I'm serving with and under. These are

things we touch on and, dare I say, in a very visceral way."

Hope And Optimism

Despite the fact that Burnham's Vulcan schooling emphasized logic over emotion, she still feels negativity towards the Klingons. After all, the warrior race was responsible for her parents' death. In the show's teaser trailer, Captain Gabriel Lorca (Jason Isaacs) tells Burnham, "You helped start a war." Could she now be seeking atonement for her actions?

"This is a story of a lot of things," Martin-Green affirms. "It's a story of failure and victory. It's a story of fear. It's a story of love and of guilt. It's a story of redemption, of restoration, and of reconciliation and of degradation. I think it's a lot of those things, but all the while maintaining the hope and optimism that is *Star Trek*.

"I truly think it's high-quality storytelling," she says. "We are able to explore all these themes simultaneously. The only reason we're able to do that is the long-form storytelling that is offered by the digital-streaming platform. That's one of the beautiful things about this

04 Georgiou (Yeoh) and first officer Michael Burnham (Martin-Green) on the *U.S.S. Shenzhou* bridge.

05 Burnham's adoptive father, Sarek (James Frain).

iteration of *Star Trek*, is that we're able to do that, that we're able to go to those darkest places while still keeping the light on, if you will. We're able to build on what's introduced into the story. Everything has ramifications. These are high-stakes consequences."

Viewers expect to be blown away by the show's production designers. Not only will the *U.S.S. Discovery* and *U.S.S. Shenzhou* take flight, but Klingon ships are ready to engage. Other settings will include the majestic bridge, impressive transporter room, and the engine room. When asked to choose the set and iconic beats that thrilled her the most, Martin-Green is almost at a loss for words.

"All of it," Martin-Green replies, in evident wonder. "I didn't know it was going to be that grand. When I walked onto the set, I was like, 'What is this? You didn't tell me it was going to be a movie every week.' I didn't realize that."

When pressed, she admits that putting on the uniform for the first time was a thrill, and says, "I love operating at my station, and pushing all the buttons. I love the phasers. I love the tricorder. I love all of it. You had these little

06

moments every day, where you're like, 'Is this real life?'"

The Alabama native's eyes light up even further when discussing one of those pinch-me moments. A sequence involves Burnham donning a space suit, and venturing into the cold vacuum of space to take it for a spin.

"Oh my gosh, my Buzz Lightyear," Martin-Green says with a big grin. "Oh man. The designs of the suit are fantastic. It was heavy, it was so challenging, but so much fun. When things are fulfilling, it's usually because they require effort. I love wirework. I love action. I love fighting. I love all of that stuff. I didn't realize I'd be doing as much of it as I am, but I love it. Bring it on."

It would be easy to assume that *Discovery* couldn't be more different than Martin-Green's *Walking Dead* gig, but that's not exactly the case. The two series feature pressure-cooker situations that put various characters' resolve, morality, and mettle to the test. And, as Martin-Green notes, "at the heart of both shows, there's a human story.

"There's a story about life," Martin-Green explains. "There's a story of the heart. There's a story that exposes the soul. In that way, they're related. All high-quality stories are related in that way. Yes, *The Walking*

06 Burnham (Martin-Green) has her suspicions about the *U.S.S. Discovery*.

"When I walked onto the set, I was like, 'What is this? You didn't tell me it was going to be a movie every week.'"

SONEQUA MARTIN-GREEN

Dead was very gritty and bleak. But, there's a lot of grit and bleakness about our show as well. There's also a lot of hope and optimism in our show, but I think you can find hope and optimism in *The Walking Dead*. You have these people sacrificing themselves for each other. The idea of family is really emphasized in that show, so that's hopeful."

Filming on location for *Discovery* is obviously impossible, so to replicate that interplanetary environment, the series relies on VFX razzle dazzle and enormous green screens. Martin-Green states she was exposed to CG on *The Walking Dead*, but not on *Discovery*'s scope or scale.

"On *The Walking Dead*, we had our knives with the little green-screen tag on it, where you had to fake the length of a knife," the 32-year-old actor acknowledges. "I'm sort of used to that combination of tactile versus imaginary scenario. I have not acted with green screen like I have now. I'm an imaginative actor anyway. I work only with imagination. I don't pull from my own life. I strictly imagine in the parameters of the story. You really have to activate your imagination when you are just staring at the green screen. If it's supposed to be this other planet, or this war going on, it's just screen. You have to picture it, visualize it, so that has been challenging."

As our conversation ends, the topic of fandom is brought up. *The Walking Dead*'s rabid fanbase routinely tunes in every week, and proceeds to dissect every development, cliffhanger, and, yes, death. So, did *The Walking Dead* prepare Martin-Green for those devoted Trekkers, who know the detail behind every quantum moment of the (currently) 700-plus hours of *Star Trek*?

"It has, in a way," Martin-Green concludes. "It's been sort of a stepping stone for me. Experiencing that show, experiencing the fanbase, experiencing the global reach of that show. I think it put me in the ball park, for sure. *Star Trek* is different. It's bigger." ⤴

EPISODE 1
"THE VULCAN HELLO"

Investigating a damaged satellite, the *U.S.S. Shenzhou* and her crew are confronted by a Klingon vessel. In an effort to prevent a war, the *Shenzhou*'s Commander Michael Burnham defies her captain, Philippa Georgiou, and tries to fire on the Klingon ship.

EPISODE 2
"BATTLE AT THE BINARY STARS"

A full-scale conflict erupts between the *Shenzhou* and Starfleet on one side, and a Klingon fleet on the other, leading to the death of Philippa Georgiou and life imprisonment for mutiny for Michael Burnham.

EPISODE 3
"CONTEXT IS FOR KINGS"

Six months into her sentence, Michael Burnham finds herself on the *U.S.S. Discovery* (whose Number One is Saru, her former *Shenzhou* colleague). The ship's captain, Gabriel Lorca, enlists her help in investigating a dangerous creature found on *Discovery*'s sister vessel, the *U.S.S. Glenn*.

EPISODE 4
"THE BUTCHER'S KNIFE CARES NOT FOR THE LAMB'S CRY"

Tasked by Lorca with studying the tardigrade creature from the *Glenn*, Burnham and Lieutenant Stamets hook it up to *Discovery*'s experimental spore drive and successfully use it to navigate a long-range jump across the mycelial network.

EPISODE 5
"CHOOSE YOUR PAIN"

Lorca is captured by the Klingons and imprisoned with a conman, Harry Mudd, and a Starfleet officer, Ash Tyler. Lorca and Tyler escape (leaving the treacherous Mudd behind), but not before the captain is tortured by the Klingon L'Rell.

EPISODE 6
"LETHE"

When Burnham's adoptive father, Sarek, is injured in an assassination attempt, Burnham connects with his mind, learning some uncomfortable truths about her adoptive brother, Spock. Meanwhile, Lorca manipulates his lover, Admiral Cornwell, into the hands of the Klingons.

U.S.S. DISCOVERY
NCC-1031

EPISODE 7
"MAGIC TO MAKE THE SANEST MAN GO MAD"

Harry Mudd returns and traps *Discovery* and her crew in a time loop, in an effort to kill Lorca and steal the ship. Along with Stamets, Burnham and Tyler foil his plan, in the process sharing a kiss.

EPISODE 8
"SI VIS PACEM, PARA BELLUM"

Burnham, Tyler, and Saru visit the planet Pahvo, hoping to use its natural crystalline transmitter to locate a cloaked Klingon vessel, but the planet's inhabitants turn Saru against the others, and broadcast a signal that contacts the Klingons.

EPISODE 9
"INTO THE FOREST I GO"

After Stamets completes 133 micro-jumps to map the Klingon ship's sensors, the vessel is destroyed. With a captured L'Rell and liberated Admiral Cornwell now on board, Stamets agrees to one last jump – but Lorca changes the coordinates...

EPISODE 10
"DESPITE YOURSELF"

Finding themselves in a parallel Mirror Universe ruled by a ruthless Terran Empire, the *Discovery* crew pose as their Terran counterparts. Burnham, Tyler, and Lorca infiltrate the *I.S.S. Shenzhou*, but not before Tyler kills *Discovery*'s Doctor Culber, who has determined Tyler has undergone surgical modification.

EPISODE 11
"THE WOLF INSIDE"

Burnham and Tyler meet the leader of the Terran resistance, triggering repressed memories in Tyler. It transpires that he is actually a Klingon who underwent surgery to infiltrate Starfleet. He is returned to *Discovery* and imprisoned.

EPISODE 12
"VAULTING AMBITION"

Burnham and Lorca are summoned to the imperial flagship, the *I.S.S. Charon*, commanded by none other than Emperor Philippa Georgiou. There, Burnham realizes that Lorca has actually been Mirror Lorca all along, manipulating events in order to return to the Mirror Universe.

EPISODE 13
"WHAT'S PAST IS PROLOGUE"

Lorca and his Mirror Universe allies usurp Emperor Georgiou, but with Burnham's help, Georgiou kills Lorca. After Burnham and the emperor beam back to *Discovery*, the *Charon* is destroyed. *Discovery* returns to her own universe – only to find nine months have elapsed and the Klingons are close to winning the war!

EPISODE 14
"THE WAR WITHOUT, THE WAR WITHIN"

Admiral Cornwell takes command of *Discovery*. The crew hatch a plan to terraform a moon, in order to grow a new crop of spores to power the depleted spore drive, and so launch a surprise attack on the Klingons' homeworld, Qo'noS.

EPISODE 15
"WILL YOU TAKE MY HAND?"

Georgiou has been tasked by Cornwell with detonating a devastating bomb on Qo'noS, but Burnham convinces her not to, instead giving the detonator to L'Rell, who uses it to unite the Klingons and end the war. Burnham is pardoned by Starfleet and restored to the rank of commander.

DISCOVERY PREMIERE

01

Stars align to welcome the new *Trek*
Words: Ian Spelling

02

The Arclight Cinerama Dome in Hollywood, California was the place to be on September 20, 2017, when *Star Trek* stars past and present gathered for the blue-carpet world premiere of *Star Trek: Discovery.*

It was a full-on affair, with the blue carpet and bright lights dazzling almost as much as the colorful costumes worn by *Star Trek* fans in attendance. No doubt the most dazzling moment of the event, however, was when *Discovery* star Sonequa Martin-Green shared a spot on the blue carpet with *Trek* legends William Shatner and Nichelle Nichols.

Martin-Green, whose luminous face conveyed the sheer magnitude of the moment, spoke to *Star Trek Magazine* moments later. "Oh my gosh,

that was phenomenal!" she enthused. "William Shatner and Nichelle Nichols! To have them both look at us and say, 'Congratulations,' and 'Enjoy it,' and to hear Nichelle say, 'It's yours now!'

"This is the first time I've met Nichelle in person," Martin-Green added. "She graciously reached out to me right after I got the job, although I was sworn to secrecy at the time. We'd only spoken online, and now we've finally met face to face."

A remarkable pop-culture event more than 50 years in the making, and a pairing of genuine social significance, Martin-Green and Nichols posed together for the massed cameras of the media, before Shatner and Nichols joined the *Discovery* cast for yet more photographs – the younger actors joyously soaking it all in.

"To be part of the opening night," Shatner told *Star Trek Magazine*, "to realize all the years that people have spent doing *Star Trek*, and watching the show, that whole careers are based on the success of this… It's really exciting."

Among those on hand were *Discovery* cast members and guest stars, including Jason Isaacs, Michelle Yeoh, Doug Jones, Mary Wiseman, Anthony Rapp, Mary Chieffo, Kenneth Mitchell, Shazad

Latif, James Frain, Wilson Cruz, Rainn Wilson, Sam Vartholomeos, and Clare McConnell. Among the behind-the-scenes *Discovery* talent enjoying the event were showrunners Aaron Harberts and Gretchen J. Berg, co-executive producer Heather Kadin, writers Akiva Goldsman, Kirsten Beyer, Ted Sullivan, Nicholas Meyer, and Jeff Russo, and make-up artists Neville Page, Glenn Hetrick, and James MacKinnon. ▶

01 Sonequa Martin-Green with Nichelle Nichols and William Shatner.

02 *(Left to right)* Gretchen J. Berg, Aaron Harberts, Heather Kadin, and Alex Kurtzman.

03 Fans gather for the blue carpet.

04 Anthony Rapp and Wilson Cruz.

05 Mary Chieffo and Kenneth Mitchell.

MORE TO DISCOVER
SEASON 2 CONFIRMED

CBS have officially confirmed that a second season of *Star Trek: Discovery* is on the way. Marc DeBevoise, President and Chief Operating Officer of CBS Interactive, said in a statement about the renewal, "This series has a remarkable creative team and cast who have demonstrated their ability to carry on the *Star Trek* legacy. We are extremely proud of what they've accomplished, and are thrilled to be bringing fans a second season of this tremendous series."

A launch date for the second season is yet to be revealed.

FAN REACTION

Along with Hollywood glitterati, a number of specially invited *Star Trek* fans joined the lucky audience at the premiere of *Discovery*'s opening episodes, "The Vulcan Hello" and "The Battle at the Binary Stars." Ahead of our in-depth review of Season 1 so far next issue, here are their first reactions to the new *Star Trek*:

"I really enjoyed it. It felt like a movie, like a cinematic movie – and this was just the first episode! The special effects were amazing; the cast was more amazing. It's the Golden Age of television, and this was prestige TV. So I'm really impressed."
DOYLE, Shanghai, China

"Visually stunning. Engrossing story. Characters are engaging, intriguing. I want to know more!"
MIKKI GUNTER
California

"It's darker, more somber, and edgier than anything we fans are accustomed to seeing. The effects and details are quite astonishing, more like a big-budget theatrical movie. At the same time, it pays homage to the *Trek* canon."
DAVID CHENG
California

"I thought it was well done. Lots to digest. Lots of good character information. Special effects were perfection. It made me want to see what happens to these characters next."
PATRYK HALL
California

"This was the *best* first episode of any *Trek* series! I enjoyed the whole episode – the cinematic look, the attention to detail, the story, and especially the interaction of the characters. *Discovery* is at once more serious and more fun than what we've seen, especially when compared to other *Trek* pilots. Our beloved *Star Trek* universe just became richer, deeper, and wider."
YEZENIA HERNANDEZ
California

06

06 Doug Jones, *Discovery*'s first officer Saru, without his Kelpien make-up.

Representing *Star Trek*'s broad spectrum and enduring legacy were a number of special guests, including *The Next Generation*'s Jonathan Frakes and Gates McFadden, the newly engaged Terry Farrell and Adam Nimoy, and actors John Billingsley, Linda Park, Robert Picardo, Roxann Dawson, John de Lancie, Nana Visitor, Anthony Montgomery, and Nicole de Boer, among others. Also walking the blue carpet were Bjo and John Trimble, credited as the fans who saved the original *Star Trek*, and the couple were obviously enjoying themselves.

Following the blue carpet, which ran for an awe-inspiring 90 minutes, everyone headed into the Cinerama Dome, where the *Discovery* cast and creatives were introduced to fans ahead of a screening of the first two episodes, "The Vulcan Hello" and "The Battle at the Binary Stars." Next, it was on to the nearby Dream Hotel for the hot-ticket after party, where Mary Chieffo (L'Rell) told us "We are so excited to finally share *Discovery* with the world."

LARRY NEMECEK
DISCOVERY: A FIRST IMPRESSION

Regular *Star Trek Magazine* columnist and lifelong *Trek* fan Larry Nemecek was at the premiere, and shared his first impressions of *Discovery*:

"My reaction that night? Must re-watch, to see how all the whispers I've been told will move the show ever closer towards the Kirk era in look, while keeping its own identify and message. Marveling at the cinematic magic, noting all the canon questions, and my own 'eh?' moments, filing away things to check later – all the while knowing that, with the incredible talent behind it, this new *Star Trek* will make a big splash in the world, just when the world needs it."

MICHELLE YEOH

TAKING
COMMAND

Michelle Yeoh has always been a force to be reckoned with. A veteran of numerous Hong Kong martial arts movies, an equal to James Bond in the movie *Tomorrow Never Die*s, and a Goodwill Ambassador for the United Nations Development Programme, the captain's chair of a Starfleet vessel was surely a destiny written in her stars.

Words: Bryan Cairns

M ichelle Yeoh looks happy as can be. With a broad grin and a twinkle in her eye, the Malaysian native's upbeat energy and enthusiasm for *Star Trek: Discovery* is written all over her face. Yeoh's role in the new series, as Captain Philippa Georgiou, commander of the *U.S.S. Shenzhou*, is clearly a big deal. Although she meets the end of a Klingon blade in Episode 2, Georgiou joins Kate Mulgrew's Captain Janeway from *Star Trek: Voyager*) as only the second female lead character in *Star Trek* to have commanded her own starship – evidence of *Discovery*'s intention to depict a future of human equality.

"In the future, there will be no distinction between race or sex," Yeoh says about the prominence of women on the show. "Anyone who is up for the job, and good for the job, gets the job. Today, I am a UNDP Goodwill Ambassador. We have 7 sustainable development goals. One of the goals we are fighting very hard for is the equality and empowerment of women. We fight the fight now, but in 200 years, that will be a thing of the past."

Yeoh's love for science fiction stems from an early age, and as a teenager she

regularly tuned in to *Lost in Space* and the original *Star Trek*. However, when Yeoh landed the coveted part of Georgiou in *Discovery*, and decided to brush up on the source material by rewatching those old series, she soon realized she had no idea what she was getting herself into.

"You suddenly think, 'Oh my God, there are over 700 episodes! How am I going to learn all of that in time?'" laughs Yeoh. "So you watch them to remind you about the essence, and how they dealt with things. Fifty years ago, when it was Captain Kirk, the stories they were telling were so amazing. They didn't have the special effects we do, they had guys running around in rubber suits, but the morals behind it, the social issues were revelant to things at that time, and this is something that will always stay. Because that is what *Star Trek* is all about, this embracing and acceptance of diversity."

Yeoh also recognizes that as a child she shared something with *Star Trek* that is integral to its appeal – the simple wonder of staring at the night sky, and the boundless possibilities of the imagination.

"Growing up, I used to go fishing with my dad, and I always looked up at

the stars at night," she remembers. "When you are sitting there, with nothing but stars, you think, 'Wouldn't it be cool if…?'"

GETTING TO KNOW GEORGIOU

Yeoh, who has decades of experience under her belt, shines brightest portraying tough, confident, and capable women. That's certainly evident in projects such as *Tomorrow Never Dies*, *Crouching Tiger, Hidden Dragon*, *Memoirs of a Geisha*, *Marco Polo*, and, of course, her latest endeavor, *Star Trek: Discovery*. Typically, writers, producers, and showrunners won't divulge everything about the character or their story arc to their actors, but Yeoh required some details to understand Georgiou, and to shape her performance.

"I had to know, where does Georgiou come from?" Yeoh reflects. "Who is she? It's not about acting and saying your lines. You have to *be* Captain Georgiou. You have to own that character. You have to make her real. The only way you can make her real is if you give her background, if you give her history. That appeals to all of us. What we are, and who we will become, is how we evolve as a human being.

01

"I sat down with [showrunners] Aaron Harberts and Gretchen Berg – who are amazing, because they've known it all for so long," Yeoh continues. "They've been working on the characters, and all the different arcs, and I asked, 'So, where is she from?' You know where she comes from geographically, because by then Earth is just 'humans,' not 'You are from the States, or from here…' Georgiou was born in the part of the world where I was born. Culturally, you would learn about the history of that place. You would see wayang dolls [shadow puppets from southeast Asia], cut out from leather on my wall. They are very traditional where I come from. It fleshes things out, and it brings you to who I want Georgiou to be."

Yeoh identifies with the optimism woven into the *Star Trek* universe, seeing Georgiou as "the epitome of that."

"She believes in the goodness of humanity, and that there is always hope," says Yeoh. "She is not cynical or jaded, even though she is a war veteran. She has seen the horrors of war, and she will do whatever it takes to never get back into that situation."

"Aaron [Harberts] came up to me and said, 'I know you can *own* that chair.' And that's exactly what you have to do. It can't overwhelm you."

CAPTAIN AND FRIEND

Set a decade before the original *Star Trek*, *Discovery* finds the Federation at war with the Klingon Empire. An accomplished warhorse, Georgiou figures in the epic conflict, but to what degree remains a mystery. However, when the series kicks off, first officer Michael Burnham (played by Sonequa Martin-Green) stands by Georgiou's side. The captain's kindness and positive attitude serves as an important counter-balance to Burnham's cold Vulcan upbringing, and Georgiou

plays an important part in Burnham's development. It's a relationship which Yeoh describes as "amazing."

"Burnham is the only human to attend the Vulcan School for Training. God forbid anybody does that, because it's quite brutal," explains Yeoh. "The way they are taught to be so singularly logical and emotionless, to know how to think, even in the worst situations. So, Burnham becomes more Vulcan than Vulcans themselves. Sarek understands that she needs to know who she is. She cannot deny who she is.

"The one person he trusted was Captain Georgiou, because of her qualities and her principles," Yeoh continues. "And when Michael Burnham arrived, she was like a solid piece of ice. Captain Georgiou and Sarek don't want to break her spirit, as she's worked so hard to be who she is. But they want her to understand that there is more than that, that it is okay to have these good emotions because they will help you, and guide you to make the right decisions. It's not just a discovery of space and looking outwards; it's also a

journey of self-discovery, especially for Burnham, to understand that if you don't know who you are, and you don't know the emotions you are able to feel, then you don't know yourself. Emotions like love, compassion, and empathy are very powerful, and help us – help the human race – overcome a lot of things. What you choose will define you as a person."

THE STAR TREK FAMILY

Over the decades, previous *Star Trek* series have enthralled audiences with exciting adventures, exotic alien races, intriguing planets, and a dash of romance. However, the heart and soul of every iteration has rested in the characters and their interactions with one another, forging strong bonds that go beyond merely being colleagues or comrades-in-arms. That hasn't changed with *Discovery*.

"They are family," Yeoh says. "You're in space for years on end. You have to watch each others' backs. Georgiou is like the head of the family, the one that will guide them. If we have

problems, she will be the one that will keep a calm head and guide us out of whatever dangers we face. You don't know what you might run into. I have a great relationship with them, because she is a character that has a sense of humor. She's not just straight-laced, like a drill sergeant. 'Do this. Do that. Get out of here.' She's not like that."

Hints at the classic trinity of Kirk, Spock, and Bones can be felt on *Discovery* as well. The clashing personalities of those three characters not only provided flashes of levity, but were the cornerstone of their loyalty and friendship. Yeoh confirms that there is something of that dynamic between Georgiou, Burnham, and Saru – and the captain delights in playing with it.

"Saru is a new species. He's a Kelpien," Yeoh explains. "His race's story is quite tragic – they were like cattle, they were bred to be eaten – and he finally stood up, and became one of the first of his species to join Starfleet and become a science officer. Saru is such an empowering figure for his species. But before Burnham joined the ship, he was already there, hoping, 'I'm

01 Georgiou goes one-on-one with T'Kuvma, in "Battle at the Binary Stars."

02 Georgiou (Michelle Yeoh) takes Burnham (Sonequa Martin-Green) under her wing.

03 Captain and first officer ("The Vulcan Hello.")

04 A date with destiny aboard the Klingon sarcophagus ship.

PHILIPPA GEORGIOU

CAPTAIN, *U.S.S. SHENZHOU*

Michael Burnham's commanding officer for seven years, Captain Philippa Georgiou of the *U.S.S. Shenzhou* was a mentor to Burnham, with whom she shared a strong working relationship and a deep personal bond.

Georgiou is a strong believer in Starfleet's peaceful mission to explore strange new worlds, new life, and new civilizations, and would rather adhere to General Order Number 1 than engage with any potentially hostile force, at least until their intentions are made clear. That determination is put to the test when her ship encounters a mysterious Klingon object, floating in the depths of space.

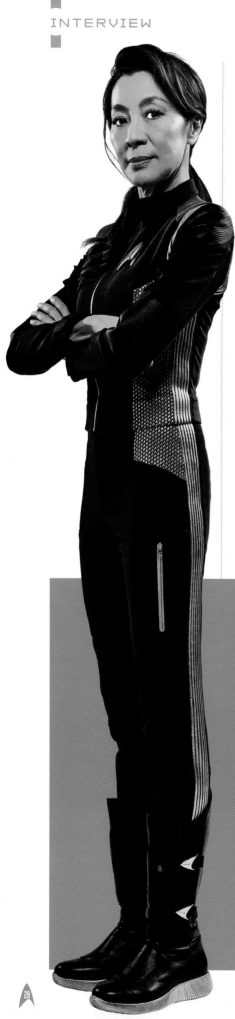

going to be the number one!' Then, he's like, 'What the hell are you doing here?'

"There's always that rivalry," Yeoh smiles. "It's obvious that Burnham has more of an edge than Saru, because of the training that she's had at the Vulcan academy and at Starfleet, so he's suddenly being relegated to, 'Oh no, I'm not going to be number one... yet!' Captain Georgiou is great. She sits back and lets them have at it. 'Okay, the two of you do it together.' 'No way. You are going to put the two of us together in a little room?' She loves doing things like that to them.

"When I sit on my chair, it's very endearing," she adds. "It's charming. It's like looking at your kids. And the way they look at you with great love and respect, it's very heartwarming."

On any given filming day, a *Discovery* scene might unfold on the bridge, in the sickbay, on a planet, or an enemy vessel. In order to pull off the wide variety of locations required, the show takes up multiple soundstages at Toronto's massive Pinewood Studios. Production design can make or break a TV series, and Yeoh can't help but geek-out over some of her favorite *Discovery* sets when asked which was her favorite.

"I don't want to say the bridge, because that's completely biased," Yeoh laughs, before settling on the transporter room. "It's so psychedelic," she jokes.

DRESSED TO IMPRESS

Costume designer Gersha Phillips spent months of trial and error in developing the signature Starfleet uniforms for *Star Trek: Discovery*. She tried out numerous colors, fabrics, and styles before perfecting the distinctive blue gear worn by the crews of the *Shenzhou* and the *Discovery*. Yeoh was extremely pleased with the end results, especially Georgiou's outfit.

"When you put on that uniform, it puts you into the posture right away," Yeoh reveals. "'Forget that extra whatever I was thinking of eating.' You can't slouch. Gersha made sure. 'You are not slouching in my *Star Trek*.' We're pristine. The costumes deserve to be seen, because the care and attention that's gone into the details are amazing. The 3D printing from Switzerland, where it's just the Starfleet emblem all across the sides... I'm like, 'Can I have just one of them, so I can frame it and put it up in my room, because it's so cool.' When you start having to move around, though, I said, 'Okay, Gersha. I think I'm going to need bigger pants.'"

"You feel like you've walked into a retro club. When Sonequa Martin-Green and I are there, we're like, 'Okay, let's start the music, man.' It's amazing.

"But, it has to be the Klingon ship," she continues, obviously impressed. "There's so much detail. The care and the creativity they put into it. It's hell to film on, because there are steps everywhere, and it's up and down. It's like when you walk into a cathedral. Everyone goes, 'Oh my God.' It's stunning."

> ## "Georgiou is like the head of the family, the one that will guide them."

Arguably the most iconic set piece of any *Star Trek* incarnation, however, remains the captain's chair. Many fans have dreamt of easing themselves into that seat, tapping away at the armrest controls while barking orders at their imaginary crews. As for Yeoh, the actress admits "it was quite daunting" when it came time for Georgiou to assume her rightful place on the *Shenzhou* bridge.

"The captain doesn't really do anything. She just sits in the chair and goes, 'You do this. You do that.' You know most of the things that are going to occur from that chair," she says, mindful of the responsibility that comes with having the best seat in the house. "But the first time you walk around it, you think, 'That's a *big* chair.' Obviously, my little short legs would be dangling from it, so luckily they have steps up to it.

"I loved it when Aaron [Harberts] came up to me and said, 'I know you can *own* that chair,'" the actor recalls. "And that's exactly what you have to do. It can't overwhelm you. This is a big chair. Then, of course, you have Captain Kirk and the way he sits. And the way Jean-Luc Picard sits, as well as the way women sit. You have to say, 'Alright, I don't want to sit cross-legged. I want to be powerful,' because you have to dominate the thing. So, I figured it out."

Dominating the chair didn't stop others from taking a turn.

"I found out something," Yeoh says, conspiratorially. "*Every* time I turned my back to leave the room, *somebody* would be diving into the chair."

STAR TREK
DISCOVERY

ON SET WITH

AARON HARBERTS

As the world waited for the launch of *Star Trek: Discovery*, showrunner Aaron Harberts took *Star Trek Magazine* on a tour of the eponymous starship's awe-inspiring sets. Along the way, he shed a little light on the creation of the show, and the story that he and co-showrunner Gretchen Berg hope to tell over the course of the first season.

Words: Bryan Cairns

"The legacy of the show is intimidating, and I'd be lying if I said it wasn't," says Aaron Harberts, addressing the pressure he and co-showrunner Gretchen Berg felt in honoring *Star Trek* creator Gene Roddenberry's vision. "There are so many hours of programming, and so many iterations of the show, and the films as well. But we knew the touchstone was always optimism, hope, teamwork and family, and using science to achieve goals. When you distill it down to that, it gets a lot less terrifying. That's got to be the touchstone, and then we built our own characters around it. We always knew that as long as we continued to hold true to a mission of hope, that we would be okay."

Star Trek: Discovery is filmed at state-of-the-art studios in Toronto, Canada, with its impressive standing sets taking up every inch of available space across several sound stages. As Harberts leads us through the *U.S.S. Discovery*'s wide, futuristic corridors, it's obvious that, visually at least, this *Star Trek* caters for a savvy, contemporary audience. With *Discovery* being a prequel to the original *Star Trek* series, we ask why Bryan Fuller and his successors decided to follow that path with the new show. Harberts notes that former showrunner Fuller was fascinated with that period in *Trek*'s future history, 10 years prior to the adventures of Captain Kirk. Furthermore, Fuller wanted to craft a story delving into the tension between the Klingons and the Federation.

01 Journalists are beamed aboard the *Discovery* engine room.

THE *U.S.S. DISCOVERY*

"This is the latest ship off the line, so the architecture reflects that," explains Harberts, as we enter the sparkling *Discovery* bridge. "It was a science vessel – a science vessel conscripted in a time of war. The bridge feels very hopeful. You stand on it and you think, 'Yeah, this is for people who are explorers, who are scientists, who are inspiring forward movement in the future.'"

02

"The touchstone was always optimism, hope, teamwork and family, and using science to achieve goals."

"There's been a lot of discussion about whether our show is dystopian or not," he admits. "I don't think it is. In fact, I know that it is not. We think of *Discovery* as a novel, as chapter storytelling. We always want people to be able to turn the page and want to watch the next episode. Sometimes that requires a large event to happen, or a loss to happen. I find when I screen the show, by the end of the episode my heart feels fuller. People are trying their best, and working through issues, and they are putting their best foot forward.

"What I truly believe, and anyone who is a fan of *Star Trek* I think would agree, is that *Star Trek* is bigger than anyone," Harberts continues. "It's bigger

"That was something that was really important to him," Harberts recalls, "so, he decided that would be the place to lodge the series, a decade before the original series. By the time Gretchen Berg and I came onboard, that decision had already been made, and we began working within that paradigm. I don't know the exact reason, but we've come to enjoy being able to pull characters from the original series, and introduce them into our timeline in a way that still syncs up with how canon represents them by the time we get to the original *Trek*.

"We never hear about Michael Burnham as she relates to Sarek and Spock," continues Harberts. "So we have to close this chapter off. We have to find the way to make sure that it syncs up with all the other iterations, otherwise it's a disaster. We already have the plan in motion."

With a second season yet to be officially confirmed, Harberts won't be drawn on what that plan might be, but it's clear that he and Berg have an eye on where the story could go.

"As we move along into Seasons 2 and 3, we can then begin thinking of ways to move into another area, to kind of pivot around. There's a huge dead end coming. We can't bash into the original series and expect the audience to take all those things in and say, 'But we've never heard about Michael Burnham.' So, figuring out why that is, figuring out why Spock doesn't mention her, are really interesting story engines for future seasons."

A NEW PATH

Harberts is keen to acknowledge the importance of the show forging its own path. Instead of chronicling

a five-year mission like that of the original *Enterprise*, *Discovery* pits the Federation against the Klingon Empire in all-out war. The idea of *Star Trek* replacing exploration with conflict has raised some Vulcan-like eyebrows, but Harberts is emphatic in his assertion that *Discovery* sings very much from Gene Roddenberry's original hymn book.

LORCA'S READY ROOM

When Lorca isn't commanding his vessel, or ordering the crew to fire on the enemy, he's busy strategizing in his ready room, located in the back of the bridge. Screens on the wall display graphics and data that keep track of the Klingon-Federation War, and the battle maps are updated with every episode. In addition, there's Lorca's standing desk, which was designed to lend the captain even more presence.

"When you walk in to greet him, he's standing," Harberts states. "He's not sitting. Immediately it adds an extra weight to a character who has tons of secrets, and a lot of mystery surrounding him.

"Jason [Isaacs] had wanted the desk to be elevated, and we thought we would put in a platform," continues Harberts. "Unfortunately, the ceiling in the ready room slopes to such a degree that if we'd put a desk upon a platform, he would have been smashing his head."

03

04

than any one of us. We're helping to guide the ship."

Like previous *Star Trek*s, which tackled real-world issues including racial intolerance and gender inequality, Harberts confirms that *Discovery* will also incorporate social commentary into its story.

"'What rights do animals have? If an alien creature, who we don't know is sentient, can help us win the war, is it fair to put that creature in pain?" Harberts offers, referring to a major plot through-line during the first half of Season 1. "How do we get around that? How do we look ourselves in the mirror? What's the debate there? When it comes to the Klingons, we need look no further than what's going on in the United States, right now. What is the logic of isolationism? What is the thing that motivates a desire for racial purity? What happens when someone is holding out their hand but the other person doesn't want to take their hand? How do you solve that problem? Can you reach peace or understanding by learning more about your 'enemy'? I think so.

"In terms of the Klingon/Starfleet war, one of our Klingons, L'Rell

[portrayed by actor Mary Chieffo], is a gigantic character within our narrative," Harberts adds. "What we want to do is tell a story about peace, but not a peace that comes from conquering the enemy. A peace that comes from both sides trying to figure it out. I don't think it's *Star Trek* to destroy to win. Winning isn't about decimating your enemy. Winning is about finding a path to commonality."

THE BRIDGE

Early concepts imagined the bridge as a multi-leveled set, but that idea was shelved due to the projected costs involved. The bridge's sleek, cutting-edge aesthetic is no less impressive despite this compromise. Hi-tech consoles, festooned with flashing lights, buttons, and controls adorn the various stations. And they look like they mean business.

Harberts notes that the display monitors on the bridge are actually future televisions, destined for retail, but originally designed by a television manufacturer for the production. The graphics that play across them are pre-programmed, so Starfleet characters can interact with them in real time, with more specific graphics being added in post-production.

Captain Lorca's beast of a chair takes center stage, with the helm and navigation stations taking up their traditional positions, facing the large viewscreen.

"Unlike other captains, Jason Isaacs made the choice to spend a lot of time up at the viewscreen," Harberts reveals. "So, you'll often see Lorca not in the chair as much as Picard or Kirk. He actually liked to play a lot of his stuff downstage."

02 Touring the costume department with Aaron Harberts.

03 Captain Lorca's standing desk.

04 The impressive bridge of the *U.S.S. Discovery.*

MICHAEL BURNHAM

The casting of Sonequa Martin-Green as *Star Trek*'s first African-American female lead garnered much press attention in early 2017. Harberts emphasizes that thinking and casting with a progressive worldview is "vital" in today's landscape.

"We had Janeway with *Voyager*," Harberts offers. "Kate Mulgrew is a super-powerful presence, and really

ENGINEERING

With its raised gantry, consoles, and that big window onto the glowing, red warp core chamber at the far end, *Discovery*'s main engineering room conjures memories of the engineering sets from *Enterprise* and the original *Star Trek*. Canisters inserted into recesses on one wall hint at Lorca's highly-classified spore-drive project (revealed in Episodes 3 and 4), as does the fortified door close to Lieutenant Paul Stamets' station.

"There are things behind that door that are quite mysterious, in terms of the technology that Stamets is developing," Harberts intimates.

THE TRANSPORTER ROOM

Harberts cites the transporter room as "another one of my favorites, because it is so iconic, and photographs so beautifully. We're in here quite a bit."

Echoing previous transporter pads, the set features the signature platform, with a bright blue color scheme illuminating the room. Off to the sides as you enter, you'll find lockers for EV suits, phasers, pulse rifles, and other essential ephemera for away teams.

"When you see our cast on the pads, you just can't help but get a rush," Harberts smiles. Interestingly, this *Discovery* set doubles as the transporter room aboard the *Shenzhou*, albeit extensively redressed. "We switch this room back and forth, between the *Discovery* transporter room and *Shenzhou* transporter room," reveals Harberts. "It is a huge switch. The transporter technology on the *Shenzhou* is different, older. The 'shower stalls,' as we call them, echo more of the original series version."

broke a lot of barriers, so we owe it to Kate. She was large and in charge on that show. But now, with what's going on in the world, and in the United States, it's important to say anybody can be in that captain's chair. Michelle Yeoh (as Captain Georgiou) is a fantastic captain of the *Shenzhou*. It's important that we realize, too, that Michael Burnham starts out as a first officer. What was most exciting for us, aside from the fact that a woman is our lead, is the fact that this is a character who thinks she knows what she wants. There's a scene in the very first episode, where Captain Georgiou says to Burnham, 'I'm going to recommend you for the captain's chair.' That's it, for Michael, who has always thought she knew how she was getting somewhere. It's all about the plans you have in life.

"By the end of the second episode, she makes choices that change her life completely," Harberts continues. "She's got to find another path. Male or female, whoever is in charge, it's a story about finding out who you are, and learning that sometimes the path you thought you'd take isn't the path you are on. I believe seeing Michael and Georgiou together sends a powerful message. It's great to see – which is not to say the male characters are getting short shrift at all. We have journeys for some of the men of the show, whether it's an alien like Saru, or characters like

CREW QUARTERS

The crew quarters of Stamets and Dr. Culber give a small glimpse into their private lives. Sheets are tightly tucked into the bed. A furry throw blanket rests at the foot of the bed, and personal items and keepsakes give the room further life.

"They're just a couple like any other couple," says Harberts. "And, for me, that meant showing a couple doing what couples do, which is why we had to do the bathroom. We do a lot of scenes of them brushing their teeth and downloading on the day, on the mission. Yes, we're saying that we have toothbrushes in 2250. So, it's like *The Brady Bunch*. There's no toilet, but I think suggestion is big enough for *Trek*."

> "What we want to do is tell a story about peace, but not a peace that comes from conquering the enemy. A peace that comes from both sides trying to figure it out."

Lieutenant Tyler and Captain Lorca, that are just as provocative."

Discovery spends a great deal of time exploring the Klingon houses, and establishes compelling new members of that infamous species. Voq, played by newcomer Javid Iqbal, was a character shrouded in mystery prior to the launch of the series. His importance to the overarching plot is yet to be truly felt, but again there are real-world parallels to the character.

"Voq represents a true believer," Harberts reveals. "In his mind, he is the Klingon messiah. It is his goal to unite the Klingon houses, who have been infighting and hurting each other. His attitude is, 'For Klingons to be great, we need to come back together. We need to unite under the motto, Remain Klingon.' That is something a lot of the Klingon houses don't care about. Voq is a true believer in T'Kuvma, and someone who is possibly going to help take up the mantle of T'Kuvma's beliefs. He represents that message, and what people will do when they believe in an ideology so strongly that they are willing to give up everything for it."

DISCOVERING STAR TREK

Star Trek's fans are legion, and devoted to the show they love. And they are also very protective of it. For *Discovery*'s showrunners, a huge challenge has been how to please existing *Star Trek* aficionados, and to connect with a new generation of fans.

"It's hard," acknowledges Harberts. "Who knows who connects with what anymore? Here's what I hope: A lot of people are introduced to *Star Trek* by their father, or their mother, or their big brother or big sister. Anecdotally, it seems like the kind of show you are guided into. Then, it becomes a lifestyle – for life. I guess the hope would be that *Star Trek* fans would turn to their kids, or their girlfriend, or whoever, and say, 'Hey, this was a show that meant a lot to me. You're my child. You're my little brother. I want to show you this.' Then it's our job to tell the kind of stories that a younger audience can get into."

In a show that's already asking deep questions of its audience, Harberts believes that the mature storytelling of *Star Trek: Discovery* has a broad, inclusive appeal.

"I think it's a very adult version of *Star Trek*," he says. "I don't mean that from the standpoint of language or nudity. We're talking about human problems. We are talking about truly discovering who you are. I think young people can relate to that. They are trying to figure it out, even though they seem super-confident, and like they have it together.

"We have some action," Harberts adds. "We have great effects. But if you don't have the emotional through-lines, and that family you are rooting for, I don't think you have a show. That's what I am most proud of. When Gretchen and I came onboard, we said, 'This is *Star Trek*, but it has got to be a family drama, and a workplace drama. People who watch have to see their lives in it.'"

05 *Discovery*'s transporter pad.

06 The ship's Engineering room.

07 Executive producer Aaron Harberts.

08 Costume designer Gersha Phillips.

09 Burnham and Tilly's crew quarters.

STAR TREK
DISCOVERY

JASON ISAACS

WAR CAPTAIN

As Captain Gabriel Lorca, Jason Isaacs delivers a compelling performance as arguably the most complex commanding officer ever to grace a *Star Trek* series. The actor reveals what drives Lorca, and why he couldn't say no to the part…

Words: Tara Bennett

Additional material: Bryan Cairns

If you're wondering what kind of man is sitting in the captain's chair for the voyages of *Star Trek: Discovery*, here's a telling moment. At the Television Critics Association summer press day for the new series, Jason Isaacs is asked, "What would Gene Roddenberry think about the new series?" Without skipping a beat, the actor offers, "He would say, 'It's the best *Star Trek* series by far!'" After a round of laughter, he adds with definite cheek, "I just spoke to him recently."

There's no question that Isaacs is coming to the venerable franchise with a supremely dry wit, and very strong ideas – and ideals – about how best he can contribute to the latest *Trek* television series. Quick as a whip, as all good Liverpudlians tend to be, the actor handles the press questions – including *Star Trek Magazine*'s – with grace, candor, and a fierce intelligence that absolutely befits the kind of personality needed to take the conn of the *Crossfield*-class starship, *U.S.S. Discovery*. And even

with a C.V. brimming with almost 30 years of stage and film roles, Isaacs is clearly taken with how fate has cast him on a series that has great personal ties for him.

"I come from a family of boys, and we used to fight, or still do fight all the time," the actor shares with a laugh. "In England when I was eight, there were only three channels, and the thing we fought most about was which channel we were going to watch at night. But there was never an argument when *Star Trek* was on. The whole family crammed onto the couch watching *Star Trek*. So the notion that I would get to stand one day and say, 'Energize,' and point phasers, and run in exactly the same way they did 50 years ago – run to the left and run to the right – because there's no CG way to look like you are being hit by a torpedo, other than an embarrassing way. It's unimaginable that we are doing it, and that we get paid for messing around like children in the backyard."

ISAACS ON...
LORCA

01

Star Trek: Discovery's Gabriel Lorca isn't your run-of-the-mill captain. A brilliant military tactician with a no-nonsense attitude, Lorca harbors plenty of disturbing and dark secrets. He's also not that warm and fuzzy with his crew, preferring to keep his distance.

Could Lorca be up to no good? Some viewers automatically pegged him as a villain. Or, in the battle between the Federation and the ruthless Klingons, perhaps Lorca is merely willing to do anything required to win the war – regardless of the cost?

Actor Jason Isaacs isn't about to spill the beans about his enigmatic character, and instead notes that, "He's not a simple man and he can't be described simply."

Explaining further, Isaacs says, "I don't believe that Lorca knows himself, and I don't know if he's consistent. I know that he's a good wartime leader. I know that he's been through some tough things. He's tough on his crew, but that's because you need people to be sharp during war. A mistake could be the end of you. He's sometimes great at interacting with people, and sometimes not. Sometimes he makes good decisions and sometimes he makes bad ones. These are richly complicated characters who change over time, and are different with different people."

DECISION TIME

Throughout his three decades as a professional actor, Isaacs is most often known for portraying complicated villains with incredible bravado, and compelling inner turmoil. From Colonel William Tavington in *The Patriot*, to Lucius Malfoy in the *Harry Potter* films, Isaacs frequently plays the man you love to hate. In *Star Trek: Discovery*, the actor even brings those ambiguous layers to Captain Gabriel Lorca of the *U.S.S. Discovery* NCC-1031.

"I'm a captain of a ship in wartime," Isaacs explains of his character. "I have people to lead, and difficult decisions to

All of the space visual effects and green screen and stuff is an added bonus, but the truth is it's an acting job, like any other – just in an interesting, long-form miniseries. And if you don't have secrets to play, you have nothing to play on camera," he smiles.

Continuing with that theme, Isaacs hints that there will be a lot of subtext with Lorca. "Nobody interesting on-camera ever says what they mean, and nobody ever fully understands themselves," he asserts. "When I've played real life characters in the past, meeting them and talking to them is completely useless. Meeting their family, their friends, their enemies, and the people they work with is the way to build up a three-dimensional picture of someone. Lorca maybe doesn't know himself, or thinks he knows himself, and is trying to do the job of a leader, which is sometimes manipulating, sometimes bullying, sometimes encouraging. And it's in a time of war. If you look at the news around us, leaders are having a tough time leading their people, and I have a tough time too."

> "Our complicated story reflects some of the complicated decisions you face when you are asking yourself, 'Do ends justify means, or the other way around?'"

VILLAGE OF THE HAPPY PEOPLE

Isaacs is also excited about the unique storytelling they'll get to explore in a *Star Trek* where war is in the now, and the future peace that audiences have come to know can hardly be fathomed.

"Nobody buys a ticket to watch the village of the happy people," the actor cracks about the wartime setting of their series. "All story is conflict. Whether I am doing a tiny, low budget movie, or a free thing for a friend who is shooting on an iPhone, or there are three cranes and a million dollars a second spent on special effects, I'm just someone standing in front of someone else, trying to get them to do something. When people use the word 'franchise,' I don't make the models or sell the bedspreads, I just tell the

make. Our complicated story reflects some of the complicated decisions you face when you are asking yourself, 'Do ends justify means, or the other way around?'"

Diving into those moral dilemmas is what Isaacs says sold him on accepting the role, even more so than his long-time affection for *Trek*. "It was the script," he says of the ultimate deciding factor. "I wouldn't play anybody who can be summed up in a sentence. Nobody I know who is interesting in real life, or onscreen, can be summed up in a sentence. So I wasn't sure whether to do it. There's no question it's enormously good fun to

dress in Lycra and fire phasers, but if I'm going to sign up to do something for as long as this, I want to know there will be something to *act*, because I don't know how to play 'starship captain.' I know how to play human beings."

He continues, "So I had a couple of very long Skype conversations with [executive producers] Akiva [Goldsman] and Gretchen [Berg]. They walked me through some of the complicated, difficult things [Lorca] does. Also some of the secrets he's got, some of the things that come to haunt him, and make him imperfect. It sounded like an acting job.

01 Lorca (Jason Isaacs) offers Burnham (Sonequa Martin-Green) a shot at redemption.

02 What is Lorca hiding in his menagerie? ("Context is for Kings")

03

ISAACS ON...
THE CAPTAINCY

When he took on the role of Captain Lorca, Jason Isaacs immediately recognized that he had big shoes to fill, following in the footsteps of distinguished actors William Shatner, Sir Patrick Stewart, Kate Mulgrew, Avery Brooks, and Scott Bakula. Their characters were defined by a morality, nobility, integrity, charisma, and wit, and Isaacs maintains that if Lorca had emerged as a carbon copy of any of the previous captains, he "wouldn't have taken the job."

"If I thought I was going to play it in any way as a shadow of any of these other actors, I would have run away, screaming," Isaacs admits. He has nothing but admiration for the actors behind *Star Trek*'s previous captains.

"I've been on screen all my professional life. This is just the next part for me," says Isaacs. "Patrick had not really done any screen work before. He was a magnificent and renowned theater actor. So was William Shatner. He was a brilliant Shakespeare actor from Canada.

"I remember looking at some of Bill Shatner's stuff," Isaacs adds. "They gave him some of the most banal dialogue, and Shatner had this gift for taking it and making it epic, making the stakes intergalactic, and being completely believable, while slightly camp. It was a genius thing that he did. I was worried about whether I could take any of this stuff and make it seem real. But, when the other actors are so good, and the sets are so real, it makes it easy."

stories, which are about people [who are] in difficulty."

With global unrest an unpleasant reality, Isaacs is also certain that this is the very best time to introduce a *Star Trek* that can be incredibly timely.

"I think we live in troubling, dark times," Isaacs says with intensity. "But we have this extraordinary prism of sci-fi and fantasy, and Gene Roddenberry's vision, to examine the craziness that's going on in the nightly news, how the world is getting more divisive, and groups are being pitted against each other. We are separating and isolating, and I don't know how to explain it to my children. I don't know how to tell them why there are people in power who say and do these awful things, and create this much division. So there's no question

03 Jason Isaacs.

04 "I glance my buttocks across it," says Isaacs of Lorca's chair.

05 Lorca encounters Harry Mudd [Rainn Wilson] in Episode 5, "Choose Your Pain."

that we are part of a story that shows not just how it can all be harmonious, but how you *get* there. We are complicated characters for complicated times, and our journey through the struggles that we have together, and where we fall out, or don't fall out, whether we make poor or good decisions, are everything the show was always about – but for the 21st Century, and for the nuanced times we live in.

"All great storytelling is 'What would you do?'" Isaacs continues. "Well, we've got some fantastic situations to go, 'What would you do? Who do you identify with?' One of the things people are saying about long-form storytelling is, when the credits roll at the end of our show, it starts the conversation. One thing about self-contained episodes is it finishes the

conversation, and then you go, 'What do we eat?'" he shrugs. "With ours, you can start the discussion with your family about who we are on the screen, but also what's going on in your life. That's the richness that you can get from a long-form story."

THE CHAIR

Isaacs is also particularly proud to be serving alongside Michelle Yeoh's Captain Georgiou, and Sonequa Martin-Green's Michael Burnham in the new series, as well as a diverse group of actors and the characters they portray.

"Just before this [series], I was in *The OA*, a show led by Brit Marling," says Isaacs. "I've got two daughters, and I couldn't be more *thrilled* to be part of a great story, told by great people, where

> "We have this extraordinary prism of sci-fi and fantasy, and Gene Roddenberry's vision, to examine the craziness that's going on in the nightly news."

ISAACS ON...
ACCENTS

Keen to avoid any comparisons being made between Lorca and Patrick Stewart's Captain Jean-Luc Picard – and to further differentiate Lorca from his other predecessors – Isaacs dropped his natural British accent in favor of a distinctly Southern States twang.

"It's a time of war," Isaacs offers. "There's something military about a Southern accent. I've trained with a bunch of American soldiers in the South. Even the soldiers from the North end up with a Southern hue to their accent. So, it has a military connotation to it, but it can be very harsh. Or it can be very charming, and seductive. And, it's not something that we've heard before from a starship captain. It was entirely my decision."

there is a woman in the lead – and see her ideas and her actions are not dictated by her relationship to men. I've been searching, ever since my girls were born, for things I can show them where I don't have to be embarrassed and explain them away."

With so much to chew on, we have to bring it back to that young kid who sat quietly with his brothers for an hour watching *Trek* on the couch, asking what it's like to actually sit in the captain's chair as the *Discovery* captain? Isaacs smirks and says, "I don't sit in the chair… as much as possible. I looked at that thing, and thought, 'It's a pit. I'm not going to sink down in it.' So, I stay out of the chair. I glance my buttocks across it, and I jump out of the thing. I actually walk up to the screen as much as I can, and I conduct war like it's an orchestra. I run around the deck, and the directors couldn't be happier, since most of the exciting bridge scenes consist of five people standing still at their stations," he deadpans. "Now, every director arrives and says, 'I hear you move?' with delight on their faces. And I go, 'I move for the right price…'"

As to his expectations for how *Star Trek: Discovery* will be received by the fans, Isaacs says, "I know the people in [our] writers' room care enormously what the Trekkies think. I *love* the ones

> "These are stories we're telling with fresh characters, and fresh dilemmas, for a fresh century."

I've met. They're great! I know they are incredibly enthusiastic. And some are enthusiastic about being furious and outraged. Some are enthusiastic because they love it. They will, all of them, even the naysayers, be in the front of the queue to watch it. I hope we give them plenty of stuff to argue about at conventions. I can't wait to get into it with them. It's made with respect and love, but these are stories we're telling with fresh characters, and fresh dilemmas, for a fresh century."

And if the series happens to change some worldviews, and maybe even some lives, so be it. "One of the things that really surprised me was meeting the people who felt that *Harry Potter* has contributed a lot to their lives, and saved their lives in some instances," he shares. "I've met a few of the *Trek* fans, and they seem to be

an incredibly passionate, fun community. They have a sense of irony about what they are doing, quite often. They don't think it's real. It reminds me of the community I met making *The Patriot*. All the people in my troop of the Dragoons were reenactors who suspended their jobs, and lived in the camp. While they absolutely lived it, and saluted me when they saw me at the supermarket, they also had a sense of fun about it. I think this is going to be a ride. Unlike everybody else, I'm thrilled there are people furious about our lens flares, or our costumes, because it just shows how much they love it all, and I can't *wait* to talk about it with them." ✦

06 Jason Isaacs as Captain Gabriel Lorca.

07 Lorca, captured by Klingons.

OH CAPTAIN! MY CAPTAIN?!

In The Neutral Zone, we present a pair of expert *Star Trek* fans with an aspect of *Trek* lore to debate, and then get them to pick sides!

This issue, we asked our duo of deliberating *Trek* fans the following question:

"Despite his ultimately nefarious intentions, could Mirror Lorca actually be considered an effective Starfleet captain?"

Loyal to Lorca:
BUNNY SUMMERS
Ready to mutiny:
MICHAEL CLARK

01

Bunny Summers: One of the absolute highlights for me in *Star Trek: Discovery* was Lorca. I found him to be such a refreshing change for a Starfleet captain, and thought he was pretty damn good at his job.

Michael Clark: Lorca cannot be considered a good starship captain. For the Mirror Universe he was most probably the most effective captain they had; he was ruthless, he took no prisoners, and he let nothing get in the way of completing his mission, no matter the loss. These are qualities that do not reflect the best in our universe of a starship captain.

BS: See, I think you're wrong. For me, Lorca is a cross between Sisko, Archer, and Janeway. He had intense drive and wanted to complete his mission like any other Starfleet captain. He was constantly pushing his crew for results; after all, this was a time of war. Didn't Sisko have to also make some questionable moral choices?

MC: Let's start with the tardigrade, a new life form found by *Discovery*'s crew. At the end of "Context is for Kings," Lorca captured the tardigrade so that he could experiment on it to help create the spore drive. The creature was tested and abused until

the spore drive worked, bringing Lorca one step closer to returning to his universe. No Starfleet captain would endanger a life form for their own means; it's a captain's job to seek out new life and new civilizations, not to cause harm.

BS: To seek out new life and new civilizations. And to protect his crew and win wars. Although we now know Lorca's war to be a different one, he's no different to other captains. The use of the tardigrade in the plot reminded me fondly of the good old *Voyager* days of "Equinox" and Captain Ransom. I believe the Klingon war

Lorca manipulated people – he manipulated the crew of *Discovery*, using their inexperience and fear of war to get them to help him achieve his goal of returning to the Mirror Universe. After convincing Stamets to use the spore drive to make 133 jumps to find a way to track the Klingons' cloaking device, Lorca then played on Stamets' desire to explore to make one last jump. With this, Lorca was able to get home. The crew were only there to serve Lorca's plans. Lorca did not inspire his crew, he did not lead them with conviction, he did not worry about his crew or if any died, he didn't care about the war. He was a selfish leader.

BS: Once again, Michael, I think you're wrong. Lorca did show loyalty to his crew. But it's important to realize that his crew were not "our" crew. We were introduced to the crew of the *Shenzhou* before *Discovery*, which I think was an interesting move. The crew was Burnham's, never Lorca's, even though they ended up on *Discovery*. While Lorca's motives were questionable throughout the season, the one thing I never doubted was his loyalty to his people – and they just happened to be Mirror Burnham and Landry.

MC: This is definitely one of those times where we're not going to agree. Perhaps it's because Lorca is not like any starship captain I'm used to that I just can't agree with you – although I'll admit I'd think twice as well before saving Harry Mudd!

BS: You know, it's a funny thing – I can't even call him Mirror Lorca. Given that he's the only Lorca we've seen, he's just Lorca to me. And I honestly do think he was one effective, badass captain, built upon a solid foundation of captain behavior we've seen before. More of that please, *Star Trek*! ↲

A starship captain would save his crew or die trying; he wouldn't run away.

in *Discovery* was no different to the survival of Ransom's crew, and Lorca did what he needed to do.

MC: "Leave no one behind" is a phrase we have heard from various ship captains, but for Lorca this meant nothing. Take Harry Mudd. In "Choose Your Pain," Lorca effected his escape from the Klingons with Ash Tyler but decided to leave Mudd behind. Yes, Mudd was working with the Klingons, but not helping him escape showed that Lorca lacked moral fiber. Lorca was the only survivor of the *U.S.S. Buran*; apparently he spared the crew from Klingon torture – or was he simply protecting himself? A starship captain would save his crew or die trying; he wouldn't run away.

Look at Admiral Cornwell. Lorca sensed that the peace conference with the Klingons was probably a trap, and when he felt Cornwell was going to relieve him of command, he convinced her to replace Sarek. She was captured, and while with the Klingons could not harm him. He didn't even try to rescue her.

BS: I'd really love to agree with you on something, but it's not going to happen. I mean, I'd like to think I'm the kind of person to leave no man behind, but if I was sharing a cell with

Mudd, I wouldn't just be leaving him behind, I'd be air-locking him for my own safety! He was being held prisoner by Klingons, and I think this was when Mirror Lorca stepped up. For this short period of time, Starfleet didn't exist; it was simply about trying to make it out with an advantage – and he got that (he thought) when he managed to escape with Tyler.

Cornwell wasn't his crew. She was just someone that Lorca had to keep in with because he needed his ship. It's unfortunate, because I consider Cornwell to be very much *my* admiral, but – she was never anything to Mirror Lorca. However, this one act does not make him a bad captain.

MC: A starship runs on loyalty; loyalty of the crew to the captain, and loyalty of the captain to the crew. Lorca did not show loyalty to his crew; only to Burnham did he show an inkling, and as we discovered, this was an obsession due to his relationship with Mirror Burnham.

01 Lorca in his ready room, in "Context is for Kings."

02 With Admiral Cornwell, in "Lethe."

03 Lorca pressures Stamets into doing his bidding, in spite of Dr. Culber's protests. ("Into the Forest I Go.")

STAR TREK
DISCOVERY

STANDING TALL...

NOT
RUNNING
SCARED

Even in a crew where self-doubt and traumatic life stories are commonplace, *Star Trek: Discovery*'s Saru stands out – and not merely by dint of his extreme height and striking appearance. By his very nature, the towering Kelpien must deal daily with his instinctual fear – something that the actor who plays Saru, acclaimed creature specialist Doug Jones, finds refreshing... even though it once again means being plastered daily with prosthetics.

Words: Bryan Cairns

01

02

I't's no coincidence that Doug Jones landed the role of the Kelpien alien, Saru, on *Star Trek: Discovery*. The 57-year-old's Hollywood calling card typically involves morphing into bizarre creatures, strange extraterrestrials, and supernatural fiends. His impressive film credits include *The Bye Bye Man* (2017), *Fantastic Four: Rise of the Silver Surfer* (2009), and a gaggle of Guillermo del Toro movies, among them *The Shape of Water* (2017), *Crimson Peak* (2015), *Pan's Labyrinth* (2006), and *Hellboy* (2004). The elaborate transformations required for those films necessitated hours and hours of being slathered in make-up, latex, and prosthetics.

At a *Discovery* press event in Toronto, Jones makes note of his growing desire to cut down on those cosmetic-heavy and time-consuming

parts. At least, that was how he felt before *Star Trek* came knocking at his door; Jones deemed the opportunity to become a part of the iconic sci-fi franchise as "special."

"To be honest, I was working on *The Shape of Water*, which is a creature movie, right before this started filming last summer here in Toronto," he recalls. "That was a head-to-toe

creature transformation. I was getting weary. That was a three-month job and I'm thinking, 'I wonder how much more of this I want to do?' Then I got offered this. I was like, 'Well, it could be six years.' We'll see when *Star Trek: Discovery* is done how much rubber-wearing I continue to do. I don't know. Never say never. I'm glad this is happening and I'm glad that *The Shape of Water* happened, too. It's an absolutely gorgeous movie, so I don't want to pooh-pooh that.

"Again, it's all about those layers and personality," he continues. "I've played so many otherworldly characters in my 30-year career so far. Saru has heart and soul. That's what will sell me on a creature now. If it's just a guy chasing you down a hallway in a horror movie, I've played those. But, they don't

"We really respect each other and would take a bullet for each other, but, gosh, Michael Burnham annoys me."

sing to me anymore. I'm 57 now and I'm getting a bit pickier. Saru sang to me. When he was described to me, I could see he had an emotional life that is very human. I can explore a lot of humanity through this alien character. That means a lot to me."

It certainly didn't hurt that Jones skipped the whole audition process. Instead, *Discovery*'s Executive Producers

01 Saru and Burnham begin to build bridges, in "Choose Your Pain."

02 Side by side in "The Butcher's Knife Cares Not for the Lamb's Cry."

03 Saru to the bridge, in "Into the Forest I Go."

TREK THROUGH LIFE

Star Trek is more than a franchise: it's a cultural phenomenon. Millions and millions of people worldwide have tuned into the show, shelled out money for the movies, bought the merchandise, or attended *Trek*-centric conventions. For Doug Jones, his admiration for *Star Trek* extends far beyond its current incarnation. In fact, he doesn't remember a time when it didn't invade his household.

"I was born in 1960, so I'm old," Jones says. "But, that also means when the original series was on network television for the first time, I was watching it. I've grown up all my life having *Star Trek* be a part of every phase of that life. There's always something on TV that is *Star Trek*-ish, whether it's *The Next Generation*, *Deep Space Nine*, *Voyager*, or *Enterprise*. And, I've enjoyed all of it."

47

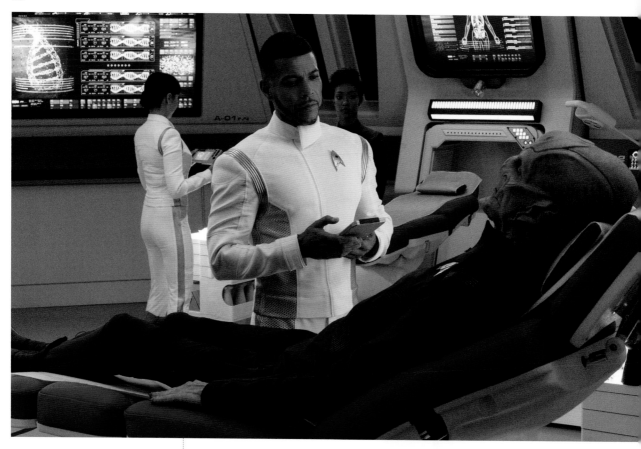

directly approached Jones about the role of Saru. Jones was "flabbergasted." But, it turns out make-up and creature designers Neville Page and Glenn Hetrick brought up Jones' name as they tinkered and toiled over the character.

"The Executive Producers happened to be fans of mine, thank heaven," notes Jones. "I went and met with them. Executive Producers Aaron Harberts and Gretchen Berg were in the room. We had a great meeting and fell in love with each other, so it was decided in that day. The gravity of what was happening was not lost on me. It just landed in my lap – and that does not just happen."

SUPERMODEL SPECIES

Over the past five decades, the various *Star Trek* TV series and feature films have introduced numerous compelling and memorable alien species. The Klingons fit prominently into *Discovery*'s first season, as do the Vulcans. However, Jones is tickled pink that Saru allows him to embody a new race of aliens rather than flesh out an already established species.

"It's very exciting, especially in such a huge franchise, with such a huge

legacy as *Star Trek*," he explains. "So many species have been birthed in this universe. To be one of them, and to be at the birthing of it, is a responsibility. I'm glad that I don't have to take on another [alien species] that has already been established because there's the chance of getting it wrong somehow. And, if I do anything wrong, the fans will be right on it. I don't blame them for that. This is good fun for me.

"The look was taken care of by Neville [*Discovery*'s Creature Designer] and Glenn at Alchemy Studios," Jones adds. "They did a brilliant job of creating this look as unique and warm and friendly. The physicality of him – what his quirks are – and the costuming came into play with my hoof-feet. I'm on the balls of my feet in a high-heel position with no heel underneath it. So, I'm balancing on the balls of my feet, like walking on a gazelle hoof. Well, that informed a lot of my physicality. It pushed my hips forward to keep my balance. I guess I got his walk down because I can't walk any other way in these boots. But, it actually works. There's a supermodel quotient to him. He walks with a certain sashay. It is with the grace of a gazelle."

04 Recovering in sickbay after the events of "Si Vis Pacem, Para Bellum."

05 Saru and Burnham in "Choose Your Pain."

06 The striking Saru.

07 (Overleaf) Doug Jones at Comic-Con.

VOICE OF REASON

On Saru's home planet, a predatory race prey on the weaker Kelpiens. Driven by fear, Saru's people developed heightened survival instincts, an acute "spider-sense" that warns them of impending danger. Saru is the first of his kind to breakaway from that life and make something of himself that's different than merely being a hunted breed.

"That's remarkable for a Kelpien to do," Jones says. "What I bring to the bridge as an officer is I'm the voice of reason. I'm the brakes. 'If you want to make a silly decision that might be dangerous,' I'm the first one to say that.

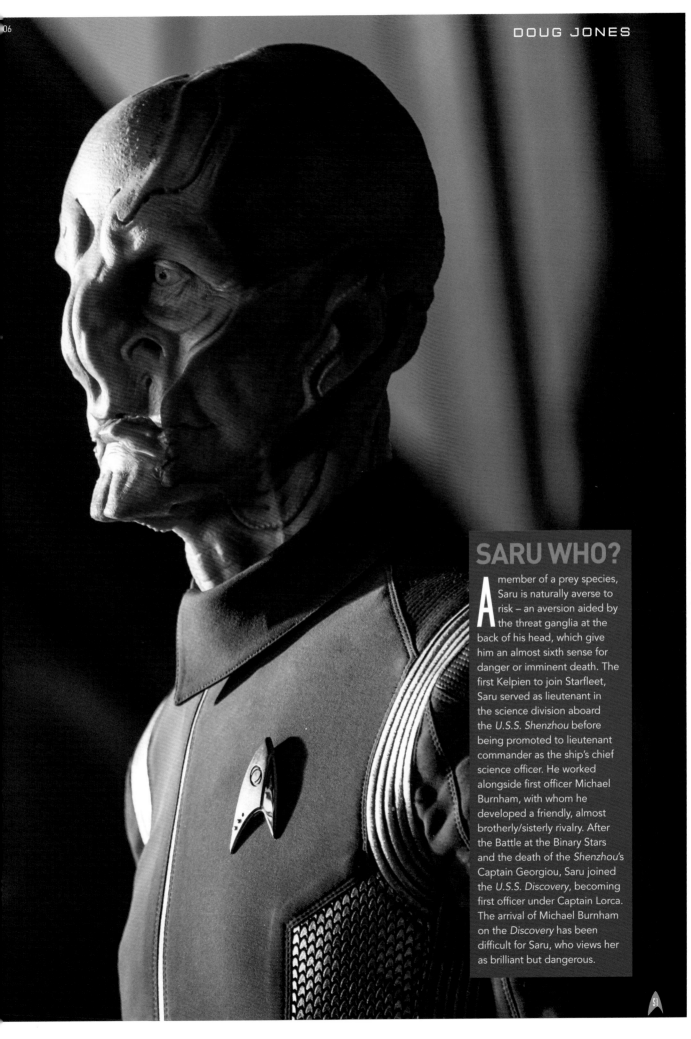

SARU WHO?

A member of a prey species, Saru is naturally averse to risk – an aversion aided by the threat ganglia at the back of his head, which give him an almost sixth sense for danger or imminent death. The first Kelpien to join Starfleet, Saru served as lieutenant in the science division aboard the *U.S.S. Shenzhou* before being promoted to lieutenant commander as the ship's chief science officer. He worked alongside first officer Michael Burnham, with whom he developed a friendly, almost brotherly/sisterly rivalry. After the Battle at the Binary Stars and the death of the *Shenzhou*'s Captain Georgiou, Saru joined the *U.S.S. Discovery*, becoming first officer under Captain Lorca. The arrival of Michael Burnham on the *Discovery* has been difficult for Saru, who views her as brilliant but dangerous.

DOUG JONES

SELECTED FILMOGRAPHY

FILM

Batman Returns (1992, dir. Tim Burton) – as Thin Clown

Hocus Pocus (1993, dir. Kenny Ortega) – as Billy Butcherson

Mimic (1997, dir. Guillermo del Toro) – as Long John #2

Warriors of Virtue (1997, dir. Ronny Yu) – as Yee

Mystery Men (1999, dir. Kinka Usher) – as Pencilhead

The Adventures of Rocky and Bullwinkle (2000, dir. Des McAnuff) as FBI Agent Carrot

Monkeybone (2001, dir. Henry Selick) – as Yeti

Adaptation (2002, dir. Spike Jonze) – as Augustus Margaray

Men in Black II (2002, dir. Barry Sonnenfeld) – as Joey

The Time Machine (2002, dir. Simon Wells) – as Spy Morlock

Hellboy (2004, dir. Guillermo del Toro) – as Abe Sapien

The Cabinet of Dr. Caligari (2005, dir. David Lee Fisher) – as Cesare

Pan's Labyrinth (2006, dir. Guillermo del Toro) – as the Faun/the Pale Man

Fantastic Four: Rise of the Silver Surfer (2007, dir. Tim Story) – as Norrin Radd/Silver Surfer

Hellboy II: The Golden Army (2008, dir. Guillermo del Toro) – as Abe Sapien/Angel of Death/the Chamberlain

Legion (2010, dir. Scott Stewart) – as Ice Cream Man

Crimson Peak (2015, dir. Guillermo del Toro) – as Edith's Mother/Lady Beatrice Sharpe

Ouija: Origin of Evil (2016, dir. Mike Flanagan) – as Marcus

The Bye Bye Man (2017, dir. Stacy Title) – as the Bye Bye Man

The Shape of Water (2017, dir. Guillermo del Toro) – as the Creature

TELEVISION

The Outer Limits (1998, 3 episodes) – as Elder Alien/Alien #1/Alien/Alien Doctor)

Buffy the Vampire Slayer (1999, 1 episode: "Hush") – as Lead Gentleman

The Neighbors (2012–2013, 6 episodes) – as Dominique Wilkins

Falling Skies (2013–2015, 27 episodes) – as Cochise

The Strain (2014–2016, 6 episodes) – as the Ancient/the Master

Arrow/The Flash (2015, 2 episodes: 'Broken Arrow"/"Rogue Air") – as Jake Simmons/Deathbolt

Star Trek: Discovery (2017–) – as Saru

Photo © Shutterstock

07

I also have a threat ganglia that comes out from behind my ears. They only deploy when a threat can't be seen, but I can sense it.

"If something is coming at me with a weapon, I can see that and [the ganglia] don't deploy because I'm ready for it," he continues. "But, if someone is behind a closed door and they are waiting to pounce on me, then I know something is not right. That's going to be the signature trait for Saru, is those threat ganglia. But, also as a prey species, when pushed into a corner, he can fight back. I do have a fierce streak in me if pushed to it.

"My threat ganglia goes off a couple of times when I'm not expecting it," he adds. "It's foretelling some kind of threat. I am also one who will say, 'Are we sure we should be making this decision?' And, if they go ahead with that decision, and it was a bad one, I have the 'I told you so.' It's also played in a humor element. The writers have been really lovely at incorporating humor for Saru, in a dry, Spock-ish or Data kind of way. It's been charming and refreshing."

PIONEERING PREY

The first Kelpien to join Starfleet, Saru served on board the *U.S.S. Shenzhou* before joining the *U.S.S. Discovery*. His upbringing informs his judgment and decision-making. It also leads him to

butt heads with fellow crew member Michael Burnham. He's cautious; she takes risks. Saru comes across as more lighthearted, while Burnham is super-serious. Their competitive nature provides an entertaining dichotomy and a "healthy rivalry."

"When you meet us right off the bat in episode one on the *Starship Shenzhou*, Michael Burnham is first officer," reports Jones. "I'm third in command, right on her tail. We are kind of like brother and sister, with Captain Georgiou as the mom figure. We have a family dynamic already. She and I are elbowing each other. We both want the captain's chair one day. We've been doing the rivalry thing all the way up to the positions we now have. There is a competition. We annoy each other, but we also revere each other. She's the smartest person I've ever known, and vice versa. We really respect each other and would take a bullet for each other, but, gosh, she annoys me."

As for what's in store for Saru, Jones prefers that audiences wait and see. Even with the Klingons plaguing the Federation, he promises plenty of room for development. "Every character is like an onion with many layers," he notes. "Each episode peels something back. You show a new color, and a new smell, that you didn't have before. Things are not always what they seem. It's a theme for the show with every character."

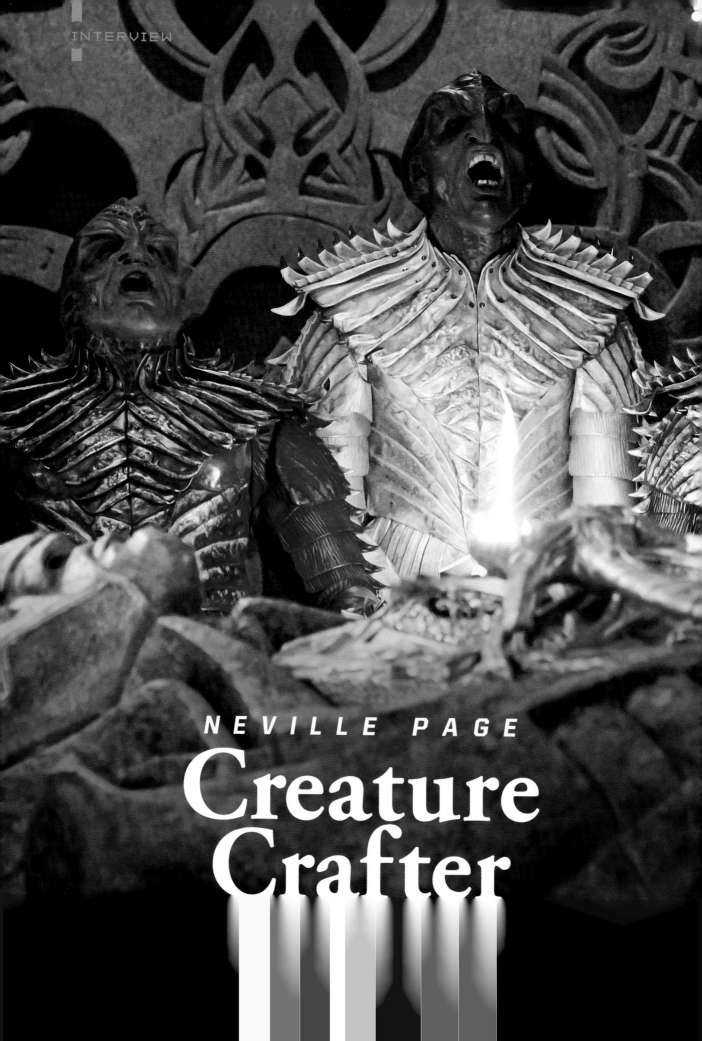

NEVILLE PAGE

Creature
Crafter

Neville Page has led a career as colorful, inventive, and unique as the creature designs and props he's masterminded for everything from *Minority Report, Avatar, Tron: Legacy, Super 8,* and *Prometheus,* to *Star Trek (2009), Star Trek Into Darkness,* and *Star Trek Beyond.* His current project is the long-awaited return of *Trek* to television, namely *Star Trek: Discovery,* for which – and not for the first time – he's been instrumental in reimagining the Klingons.

Star Trek Magazine recently caught up with the enthusiastic Page, who filled us in on his experiences on the three *Trek* features, and how he beamed aboard *Discovery.*

Words: Ian Spelling

Star Trek Magazine: What led you to become a creature designer, and who were your earliest influences?

Neville Page: My parents were entertainers. My dad was in the circus as a drummer, and my mother was a dancer in the theater, in London. So, entertainment was always a part of the ambient noise in my life as a child. My grandfather was a musician; my mother's father, he was a painter. Art and expression were always allowed. It wasn't something that was stifled, but it was not something that my parents wanted me to do professionally, because at age five, when we moved from England to the States, it was a goal for the family to do better. It's not as if my parents wanted me to become a musician or a dancer. And, oddly, I aspired to do both of those. I actually trained to do both of those.

Then you discovered Rick Baker and Star Wars.

> "I presented my design to Justin Lin, the director, and he said, 'That's her. That's Jaylah.'"

Those two things, and also Frank Frazetta [the renowned American fantasy and science fiction artist]. I found his book at a garage sale. It's *The Fantastic Art of Frank Frazetta*. I still have it. The price tag from the garage sale is still on it, but there's no price you can put on it for sentimental value. Seeing *The Fantastic Art of Frank Frazetta*, and then seeing *Star Wars*, and then seeing Rick Baker, whose work was starting to be showcased in *Fangoria* and *Starlog* magazines all the time, all made an impact on me. I remember this one picture I saw of Rick Baker with a clay

01 *Discovery* introduced a new look for the Klingons.

02 Sofia Boutella as Jaylah, in *Star Trek Beyond*.

03 Page's Klingon make-up for *Star Trek Into Darkness*.

04 The palid look of the Nibirans was Page's first challenge on *Into Darkness*.

05 T'Kuvma (Chris Obi).

sculpture of Mr. Hyde. When I saw it as a 10-year-old, I thought, "Human hands squeezed clay to look like that? That's unbelievable to me." I was hooked. It's so great to know Rick personally now, and talk about that moment.

So at that point in your life, *Star Trek* wasn't on your radar?

No. I had aspirations of being on the set of *Star Wars*. I wanted to wear Luke Skywalker's costume and have a lightsaber. I thought, "How do I actually do that? Clearly *Star Wars* isn't a real-life opportunity, so maybe I should get into film as actor. Then I can wear the costumes, and roleplay on film." I moved to California to become an actor, and studied at the American Academy of Dramatic Arts, which is a great, reputable school, and became, in quotes, an actor. That meant I worked at several restaurants in Los Angeles and auditioned a lot, and got… nothing. I started to realize, "I don't get to exercise the craft. I truly like the craft of acting, but I'm not getting to do it." If I was in a commercial, I was like, "Ah, it's not really acting, and I'm certainly not holding a lightsaber." So, I bailed. I thought, "Let me go the route of design."

I'd heard of this school called The ArtCenter College of Design in Pasadena. I wanted to go there because of my knowledge of the guys on *Star Wars*, like Joe Johnston, Ralph McQuarrie, and Nilo Rodis-Jamero. Those three guys were educated either as illustrators or industrial designers, so I went the industrial design route. That's how I got into doing medical products. Thinking I was going to do film when I graduated, I fell in love with this whole idea of engineering and designing consumer goods. So, that's what I did for many years, working for BMW, and also

04

"Bryan Fuller loved the engineer from *Prometheus*… He thought, 'That'd be perfect to have as an inspiration for our Klingons.'"

05

some cool automotive companies and high-end aerospace companies. I lived in Switzerland for a couple years, teaching.

What was it that led you and your business partner at the time, Scott Robertson, to move back to the States?
We had an opportunity to reimagine ourselves, so we said, "What do we want to do?" He started a publishing company, and I thought, "I'm going to somehow get into film." I'd designed wheelchairs for so long that I was handed the project to do the vehicle for the *Men in Black* ride at Universal, *Men in Black: Alien Attack*. Phil Hettema was the man in charge of the ride. They needed it to be wheelchair-accessible. I thought, "But this is *Men in Black*. I'm a fan – is there any way you'd let me design a creature too?" They said, "Well, you don't design creatures but go ahead and draw a couple." I was successful enough to have them be interested in me managing almost all creatures for the ride. That's where I met these incredible artists who became, unbeknownst to them, my mentors. Carlos Huante, Jordu Schell, Jose Fernandez, Jim Kagel. These guys were working in my shop. They were the top guys in Hollywood at the time, and still are. Those were my teachers, and they were my exposure to creature design. I thought, "That is what I aspire to do and become."

What was the stepping stone that set you to work with J.J. Abrams on the 2009 *Star Trek* film?
Minority Report, the Spielberg film. Well, it started off with *Men in Black: Alien Attack*, because Steven was one of the movie's producers, and he was involved with the ride. We had to present to him and have him approve stuff, so I met Steven. Then

one day there's a knock at my studio door – a woman saying somebody had left their keys at my studio. She looks in our studio, and says, "You guys do helmets." We did. We did a lot of bicycle helmets and hockey helmets, so I said, "Yeah." She said, "Oh, I'm working on a movie called *Minority Report*, and we need some gear and some helmets. Would you mind being a part of it?" I said, "Not at all. What's your name?" She said, "Colleen Atwood." I said, "OK, I don't know who you are, but we'll give you a hand." I didn't realize that she was *the* Colleen Atwood, such an amazing, accomplished, Oscar-winning designer.

And you found yourself on set again with Spielberg?
Steven, who is a genius guy and who should not remember me, remembered me from the *Men in Black* project. It became more familiar. Why I'm sharing this is just how full-circle all of this can be. After doing *Minority Report*, there was an opportunity to do *Planet of the Apes* with Colleen, and facilitate some of the costume work on that film. So, I'm starting to get a couple of things on my résumé, but nothing of significance as a creature designer. I was still an industrial designer dabbling in film.

Then along came *Avatar*…
Exactly. I get the call from a buddy who's working with James Cameron, who says, "Jim's looking for artists to do creatures for his film called *Project 880/Avatar*." I thought, "Well, you don't ever win the lottery unless you buy a lottery ticket. I don't have much creature design work, but let me try." I was selected, with three other guys, to work at Jim's house for a couple months to draw a few ideas. That turned into a three-year project. During the course of that, I got a call from J.J. Abrams saying, "Hey, I'm

07

working on this interesting project called *Cloverfield*, which is going to be a very different approach." *Avatar* was not out yet, and was not going to be out for several years. J.J. found me via the Gnomon School of Visual Effects. I'd made some DVDs on drawing and other techniques, and J.J. said, "I saw those DVDs, and I thought they were cool. Do you want to work on this film?" I'm thinking, "This is bizarre," but that started the relationship with J.J. At the end of *Cloverfield*, it rolled into *Star Trek (2009)*. That was a small gig that turned into a year-long project. And then, all with J.J., I did *Super 8*, *Star Trek Into Darkness*, and *Star Trek Beyond*.

Which of the creatures that you designed for *Star Trek (2009)* were you most satisfied with?

I was hired specifically to do the big red creature. Only, when I was hired, it was not a big red creature. The scene was set on a desert planet and, as described, it was a dragon-like, bat-like, multi-eyed turtle thing. I thought, "This is cool. I get an opportunity to work on a creature." Then, the script changed and it was an ice planet, so that meant I was designing the wrong thing. One of the greatest things about working with J.J. is his propensity for collaboration. J.J. invites you to participate

"One of the greatest things about working with J.J. is his propensity for collaboration."

in the process in the course of him trying to realize his vision. I said, "Would you mind if I proposed something about the ice planet creature?" He says, "Go ahead. What do you have?" I said, "OK, let me do some storyboards. I have an idea for something."

It involved pulling a red herring trick instead. You see something on surface, that we called a Polarilla, racing towards Kirk. You think that's the scene, and then all of a sudden this thing comes through from underneath. The underneath part is critical, because the creature was never intended to be on land. It's an underwater creature, much like a Humboldt squid meets a lobster. J.J. was specific – big, red, lots of eyes. It's a massive predator. I thought, "Well, if he's chasing Kirk, he's going to be able to catch him easily, so if we literally make him a fish out of water,

06 Page designed the Polarilla, and the "big red creature" which pursues Kirk across the frozen wastes of Delta Vega, in *Star Trek (2009)*.

07 *Discovery* offered Page his third opportunity to redesign the Klingons.

then it gives Kirk the opportunity to get some distance." If you're being true to biology, morphology, and to the narrative, then you know what to do with a design, as opposed to, "Here's a cool shape. Let's see how we can shoehorn that into the process." You make those decisions. The big red creature was so much fun to explore, and it was fun to play with and collaborate with J.J., and to arrive at something he felt was cool.

How different an experience was *Star Trek Into Darkness* versus *Star Trek (2009)*?

It was very similar because it was the same writers, it was the same cast, for the most part, and J.J. was directing again. It was the same family. I remember when Jeffrey Chernov called me up, he said, "Hey, we're getting the band back together." I thought, "Oh, cool." These productions are just like that. They become family. The make-up artist was different – Joel Harlow was busy with Johnny Depp, as he often is – so Dave Anderson was the make-up lead. He's a sweet, charming guy, equally as talented, in different ways. That was maybe the only big difference.

Dave Anderson's partner is Heather Langenkamp, who played a funky alien

THE TORCHBEARER

Making a memorable if all-too-brief appearance in *Star Trek: Discovery*'s debut episode, "The Vulcan Hello," the symbolic battle armor worn by the Torchbearer was conceived as a sophisticated EV space suit. Built in Los Angeles by Neville Page and Glenn Hetrick's Alchemy Studios, cutting-edge 3D printing techniques were employed in the creation of the Torchbearer armor, and the finished piece was made up of 100 individual, digitally-designed components.

"I really wanted to do something that you just can't do normally," Page told *Star Trek Magazine* of the techniques used to realize this striking design. "You can't handsculpt those shapes, symmetrically, within the time and money. I thought, 'This is a really great opportunity to do something that's so visually complex.'"

09

08

in *Star Trek Into Darkness.* **She's famous for the *Nightmare on Elm Street* movies.**
Exactly! It was so funny when we were meeting everyone at the beginning. [Heather] was Dave Anderson's shop manager, so it was me, her, and Dave waiting for J.J. as we always do. Then J.J. comes in and geeks out over her. He's all, "Oh, my God! I can't believe I'm meeting you!" It's funny how that is. We're all fans of someone.

But *Into Darkness* was no different from the first one, other than the challenge of the Nibirans. That was a moving target. Day one, they were the first thing that I started to work on. It's a privilege when you start on a project that early as a designer – it's always a privilege – but the negative is that the script isn't done. It's being developed. So, you get excited

about a scene you're designing and then the scene is written out. You think, "But that was such cool stuff!" It's delusional to think everything you're doing is about you. It's not.

In *Star Trek Into Darkness*, you were able to take on the Klingons. How was that?
We'd had them in the first *Star Trek*, but they ended up being in helmets, and then those scenes got cut. J.J. said, "We're going to do it this time, but one of the helmets is going to come off, maybe in a fight, maybe in a reveal." Which meant we got to see Klingons, for the first time in a long time.

J.J. asked, "What are we going to do with them?" I thought, "Well, can we make the Klingons – and no offense to previous Klingons – can we make them sexy?" That was my personal ambition. Let's make them as tough, as warrior-like as possible, but like they're beautiful, powerful beings. I went into it with that goal. We explored some beautiful range with them.

What was the standout design for you from *Star Trek Beyond*?
Jaylah. We didn't know what that was going to be at all. We didn't know who the actress was. There was a lot of hunting for what that could be. In one quick moment, I did a Photoshop illustration of that graphic [of Jaylah's distinctive face markings], and that was it. I thought, "That has the potential to work." The reason I like that look so much is because it's strong. It's black and white. You can't get stronger graphics. I presented the design to Justin Lin, the director, and he said, "That's her. That's Jaylah."

10

> "I felt *Discovery* would be a great opportunity to utilize all these 3D modeling and 3D printing technologies."

You could destroy a design with the wrong casting – we're not involved with casting, we're only involved with, "Here's a basic design" – but because it's on Sofia Boutella, she has a face that is so perfect for it. It really was a perfect marriage.

Given your *Star Trek* résumé, were you expecting the call to work on *Discovery*?
Alex Kurtzman brought me on. He and I have a good relationship, so I wasn't surprised at the onset. I believe it was because of a conversation that Alex and Bryan Fuller were having about the Klingons, about what they were going to look like. Bryan was crystal clear that he

08 The Klingon EV armor worn by the Torchbearer.

09 Mary Chieffo's L'Rell set the template for Klingon's new look.

10 Racks of Klingon armor in the *Discovery* costume department.

11 Lorca and L'Rell in "Choose Your Pain."

loved the engineer from *Prometheus*, not only because of it being the engineer from *Prometheus*, but also, I think, because of the H.R. Giger influences. He thought, "That'd be perfect to have as an inspiration for our Klingons." As I'd worked on *Prometheus* and did the engineer, it made sense.

So this was a unique third opportunity to develop Klingon morphology?
It started with the Klingons and the Sarcophagus Ship, and with Klingon world-building. Initially it was not the 24 houses. We spoke about the houses, but that's further down the road. It was not initially that big a world. Once we got the

morphology of the Klingons figured out, manipulating that into the other houses would be developed as needed. It is a budgetary thing. Every house has a price tag in development.

Because of my interest in costume design, and coming in from *Tron*, *Oblivion*, and a few other films, I felt *Discovery* would be a great opportunity to utilize all these 3D modeling and 3D printing technologies that we've used in a few films, but we haven't used in this capacity on TV. So, I came in, guns a-blazing, to meet with Bryan Fuller, Aaron Harberts, and Gretchen Berg. I had literally a bag of 3D printed parts, and some images of Klingon armor with our new Klingon designs, and said, "If you don't use me, you still have to use this technology, because it will yield stuff that we've not seen in very many major films, and we've never seen on a television budget."

Is it your hope to stick with *Discovery* for as long as it runs?
The opportunity to continue designing creatures, to start to populate these worlds, I would absolutely love to do that. It's a very rich world, with a lot of old and new stuff to play with. ⬆

11

STAR TREK DISCOVERY

SHARED QUARTERS

STAR TREK: DISCOVERY'S HAPPY COUPLE

Star Trek's reputation for embracing diversity and pushing social boundaries has been there since the very beginning, and continues in *Star Trek: Discovery*. When the latest *Trek* TV series premiered on September 24, 2017, it had already garnered plaudits for featuring the first African-American female leading role in the franchise's 51-year-old history. Not only that, but it also introduced *Trek*'s first openly gay regular characters, the spiky scientist Lieutenant Paul Stamets, and his partner, Doctor Hugh Culber. *Star Trek Magazine* spoke to Anthony Rapp and Wilson Cruz, the actors behind *Trek*'s groundbreaking couple about their respective roles.

ANTHONY RAPP

LIEUTENANT PAUL STAMETS

Words: Bryan Cairns

"I have a friend – one of my best friends – and he's a huge Trekkie," says Anthony Rapp, addressing the importance of LGBTQ visibility in *Star Trek: Discovery*. "Before I ever knew him, he was going to conventions when he was a kid. He was doing fan letters and newsletters. He's gay, and he's been very aware of the sizeable LGBTQ community within *Star Trek* fandom, so he's been one of my touchstones through this experience.

"He's enormously proud and excited to see that this is finally happening," Rapp continues. "It's meaningful to me on so many levels. The fact that I have a close relationship with a friend, who is also greatly affected, is incredibly meaningful."

From the start, the intention of *Discovery*'s producers was to make Stamets and Culber's relationship absolutely relatable to everyone. Run-of-the-mill, even. The pair have a recognizable domestic life when not on duty, sharing the same living quarters, and brushing their teeth together at the end of the working day. (Yes, Stamets' reflection spookily remains in the bathroom mirror after he's walked away, but that's beside the point...)

"I'm really honored, and proud, to get to carry that particular flag," Rapp says. "The fact of my character's sexual orientation is just one facet among many others, and is treated as simply and straightforwardly as any other."

However, the two characters must also navigate their jobs, separating their personal lives from their professional duties. For Stamets, that's science, and his explorations in the field of astromycology. His forte is space mushrooms. "I am possibly exposing myself to dangerous things," Rapp notes, wary of exposing plot spoilers ahead of *Discovery*'s January return to CBS All Access, but it's clear during the first half of Season 1 that Stamets' research could ultimately tip the scale in the Federation's war against the Klingons.

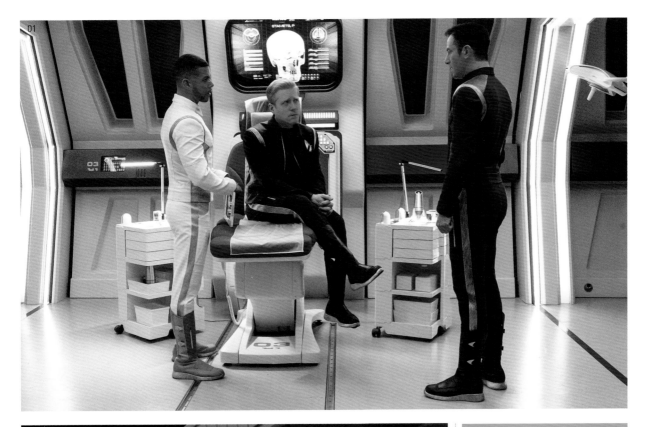

01

02

RAPP ON STAMETS

"I wouldn't call Stamets an introvert," Rapp reflects. "I wouldn't call Stamets warm and fuzzy. He's prickly. He's super-smart, and doesn't suffer fools, and doesn't have time to deal with the minutiae – 'The question you're asking me is not nearly as important as the question I am asking myself' kind of thing. So, he's not introverted. He's definitely able to have a conversation."

"There's extra pressure coming from my captain, because my project is important to the mission," Rapp says. "The pressures that he's putting me under are possibly challenging my well-being, because of what I'm having to deal with."

THE MUSHROOM MAN

One of the stranger concepts to be explored in *Star Trek: Discovery* has been the notion of the mycelial network, the universe-spanning root system of the fungus *Prototaxites stellaviatori* that Stamets navigates when operating *Discovery*'s Spore Drive. The concept is rooted in a real-

world theory, so out-there that it almost pushes the boundaries of science fiction. What's more, it was proposed by a real-world scientist named Paul Stamets, from whom Rapp's character takes his name.

"It's been very cool to dip my toe into the real Paul Stamets' research on mycology," says Rapp, "and the implications of these microorganisms – mycelium – that grow into the fruits that are called mushrooms. They have far-reaching applications in our world, and there has been really interesting research about how it speaks to all sorts of natural systems of our world, and therefore the universe.

01 Is the spore drive causing long-term damage to Stamets' health?

02 Anthony Rapp as Lt. Paul Stamets.

"This microscopic stuff can actually expand the way we view things," Rapp continues. "That is a real level of discovery that has far-reaching implications in how I see the universe. I'm not being hyperbolic. On a micro-level, I'm a scientist, so when I encounter Sonequa Martin-Green's character [Michael Burnham] for the first time, I file things away. Then, of course, I discover there's much more to her than at first glance. Same with Cadet Tilly, and Captain Lorca. Throughout the whole series, there's tremendous growth and change in how we all interact with each other."

CAPTURING THE IMAGINATION

Star Trek Magazine has spoken with many of the *Discovery* cast, and it has been crystal clear that the *Star Trek* legacy resonates with them all in some unique way. Rapp is no exception. The Chicago native vividly recalls his favorite *Trek* character, and has fond memories of the original series.

"When I was a kid, I was watching the reruns. I remember the music, I remember the movies, I even remember the posters, and the bugs crawling into Chekov's ear in *The Wrath of Khan*," offers Rapp with glee. "But Spock was the character that always captured my imagination the most, as a kid."

Rapp is also keen to sing the praises of *Star Trek: The Next Generation*'s Jonathan Frakes, who returned to *Star Trek* to direct an episode of *Discovery*'s second tranche of stories. Frakes, who portrayed Commander William T. Riker across seven seasons of *TNG*, four feature films, and the final episode of *Enterprise*, had been extremely vocal about his desire to be involved with the new show.

"Jonathan totally embraced every aspect of it," Rapp enthuses. "This thing that he was a part of meant so much to so many people. Some people, when they are in that situation, feel trapped by it. They want to walk away from it, but he's totally embraced it. It hasn't stopped him and he's not stagnated by any means.

"It's been very cool to dip my toe into the real Paul Stamets' research on mycology."

He's gone on to continue to do really good work. For him to come back, and be a part of our version of *Star Trek* was meaningful.

"Just technically, what he has at his disposal as a director – with the cranes, and the Steadicams, and the sets, and the visual effects – he has gratitude for that latitude," Rapp continues. "And, Jonathan felt that our camaraderie as a cast was very familiar to him. We have become family immediately. Where that family aspect comes from is being there together, in the trenches, taking care of each other, and wanting to take care of each other."

Indeed, Rapp is grateful for the bonds he's forged along the way.

"You never know what it's going to be like," Rapp concludes. "There's the long hours and the challenging material, but I think they've done an incredible job of casting people who are good human beings, and care, who want to do their best work. There's big shoulders to stand on, and a lot to honor. We're doing our very best to do that."

03 Rapp hits the publicity trail at San Diego Comic-Con.

04 Culber (Cruz) and Stamets (Rapp) take time out with Tilly (Mary Wiseman).

05 Rapp and Cruz at the *Discovery* premiere.

CREW MANIFEST

ANTHONY RAPP

Best known for originating the part of Mark Cohen in the 1996 Broadway production of *Rent*, Anthony Rapp is a well-established theater, film, and television performer, whose professional career stretches back more than 35 years.

Born in Chicago, Illinois in 1971, the young Rapp sang from an early age, and made his first appearance on Broadway in 1981 in *The Little Prince and the Aviator* – a musical that closed during previews. Undeterred, Rapp starred in numerous Broadway and off-Broadway shows before making his feature film debut in *Adventures in Babysitting* in 1987. More films would follow, including 1993's Richard Linklater-directed coming-of-age comedy *Dazed and Confused*, 1996 disaster movie *Twister*, and Ron Howard's Oscar-winning movie *A Beautiful Mind* in 2001 (for which *Discovery* writer and director Akiva Goldsman won Best Screenplay).

Other notable stage performances include 1999's *You're a Good Man, Charlie Brown*, 2003's *Hedwig and the Angry Inch*, and the musical *If/ Then* in 2014. Rapp starred in Chris Columbus' movie adaptation of *Rent*, and reprised the role of Mark Cohen again for the renowned stage musical's 10th anniversary revival in 2006.

WILSON CRUZ
DOCTOR HUGH CULBER

Words: Ian Spelling

Wilson Cruz, back in 2009, played a character named Sid Tango in "Kerplunk," an episode of the acclaimed, albeit sadly short-lived television fantasy *Pushing Daisies*. Cruz now plays Doctor Hugh Culber on *Star Trek: Discovery*, and he can directly thank "Kerplunk" for helping him book a place on the final frontier.

"I've never talked about this, but when it was first announced that Bryan Fuller was heading up the new *Star Trek* series, I reached out to him because I had worked for Bryan in the season finale of *Pushing Daisies*, which was an episode that Aaron Harberts and Gretchen Berg actually wrote," Cruz tells *Star Trek Magazine*, after wrapping up the *Discovery* actors panel at *Star Trek Las Vegas 2017*. "So, I knew Bryan, Aaron, and Gretchen from doing that. I reached out to Bryan and said to him, 'Hey, if there's anything that's appropriate for

me, I would really love the opportunity to be on the new show.' He was, like, 'I think that's a great idea. I would love to see you in that.'"

Unfortunately, a giant wrench was thrown into the works when Fuller departed *Discovery* well before it came time to cast Doctor Culber, who would serve as the medic aboard the *U.S.S. Discovery* and be romantically involved with Lieutenant Paul Stamets. When casting time did roll around, the producers hired Anthony Rapp to play Stamets, and Cruz touched base with them to praise their "awesome" choice, telling them "how much they were going to love Anthony." Cruz and Rapp, it turns out, were old friends and had overlapped briefly in the popular Broadway musical, *Rent*.

"I also said to them, 'It would be cool to work with Anthony again,'" Cruz recalls. "It was something like that, and I never heard from them – but then I got offered the role of

CRUZ ON CULBER

08

"I love Culber. I love him because he is dealing with a few things," Cruz enthuses. "Like everyone else on this show, he's a genius. He is at the top of his field, and so I have great respect for that. He is also a soldier. I drew inspiration from actual doctors and nurses on the battlefield, who are dealing with the fact that they have to help the mission and be sure that the mission succeeds, but also need to be keenly aware of the health and well-being of their fellow crew members, and being responsible for that.

"Then, there's the added element of being in love with a person who is also part of your crew, and how he walks this fine line between being ultra-professional and great at his job, but also how the love he shares with Paul makes him question things he wouldn't ordinarily question," Cruz continues. "I love this internal battle that he has, on a number of levels."

▶ Doctor Culber. There was some back and forth with the network, and they wanted me to do a screen test. When I showed up to that screen test, Aaron and Gretchen said, 'This is our reply to your call.'"

Cruz, who is gay and a vocal advocate for LGBTQ causes, has played gay characters before, including one of television's first gay series-regular characters, Rickie Vasquez, on *My So-Called Life*, with the character becoming a fashion icon in the process. Now, Cruz is helping break new ground as half of a *Star Trek* series' first gay couple.

"That's just... beyond for me," Cruz marvels, a joyous smile barely masking tears of joy. "It really is. So many of us have waited to see this on *Star Trek*. What it says to young people watching it is that when the future comes, we will be a part of that. LGBTQ people have always been a part of civilization, and to see that we will continue to be a part of civilization is incredibly important. For a young person to turn on the television and be able to see themselves is really important, too. It was the characters on TV and in film that allowed me to dream outside of what was expected of me, that really freed me of those expectations, and allowed me to

> "For a young person to turn on the television and be able to see themselves is really important."

dream bigger dreams for myself. So, if Anthony and I can do that for a young LGBTQ person, then we will have fulfilled a great need."

GETTING TO GRIPS WITH MEDIBABBLE

Cruz is equally enthusiastic when asked about the show's massive, incredibly detailed sets,

"The sets are so immersive. My imagination goes wild," he says. "I'm so grateful to the crew that built all of our sets, because it does 75 percent of the work for you. When you walk onto the bridge or into the med bay, you're automatically transported into that world. Though I have not beamed up," adds Cruz, with slight disappointment. "Or down."

During the *Discovery* actors' panel earlier on the day of this interview, Cruz could barely wrap his tongue around the word "hypospray," so it seems fair to ask how he is dealing with *Trek*'s infamous technobabble – or "medibabble," in Doctor Hugh's case. Cruz notes that as he reads each new script on his tablet, "I have my computer open to a medical dictionary, a science dictionary, and a regular Merriam-Webster dictionary, because I don't know half the words that I have to say!" Laughing at himself,

Cruz admits, "Everyone thinks that none of the words in *Star Trek* are real, but that's not true. Everything that I've had to say is based on something very real. They might take it to another level, but it's all based on something very real. It's been educational for me to learn some biology and anatomy, and urology, and physiology, for this show. It's been really educational in that sense, but, honestly, when we're done with the scene, it's like a valve opens up in the back of my head and it all spills out, because I have to make room for the next scene and the next crazy medical terms. It has been a challenge. I'm not going to lie!" ✦

08 Dr. Culber (Wilson Cruz) monitors the health of Lt. Stamets, during another dangerous spore drive jump.

CREW MANIFEST

WILSON CRUZ

Wilson Cruz was born in Brooklyn, New York, and grew up there and in California. His parents are of Puerto Rican descent. Cruz started acting in plays when he was just seven years old, and he was studying both theater and English at California State University at San Bernardino when he landed his breakthrough role on the television series *My So-Called Life*. Though best known for that role, and for appearing in the musical *Rent*, his many other film and television credits include *Nixon*, *Joy Ride*, *Party Monsters*, *He's Just Not That Into You*, *Mistresses*, and *13 Reasons Why*.

STAR TREK DISCOVERY

THE ALCHEMY EFFECT

The makers of *Star Trek* have always embraced cutting-edge production technology, breaking new ground on television and in cinemas with visual effects, prosthetics, and the use of high-definition photography and digital post-production. The latest television incarnation, *Star Trek: Discovery*, is no exception, thanks in large part to the multi-discipline effects team at Alchemy Studios. *Star Trek Magazine* spoke to the company's founder, Glenn Hetrick, to find out how the very latest techniques helped bring the new show to the screen.

Words: Joe Nazzaro

Alchemy Studios evolved from Glenn Hetrick's previous, Emmy award-winning enterprise, Optic Nerve FX Inc., in response to the changing landscape of cinematic visual effects work. Known for his incredible make-up prosthetics on shows including *Babylon 5*, *Buffy the Vampire Slayer*, and *The X-Files*, Hetrick recognized that emerging technologies, including 3D printing and the possibilities of closer integration with CGI, could take his work to another level.

With previous TV versions of *Star Trek*, alien make-up design was largely confined to a humanoid physique, with more exotic and unusual features confined to the face and head. While *Enterprise* pushed that envelope, the *Kelvin* Timeline films relaxed those long-standing restrictions of what could and couldn't be done with *Star Trek*'s alien designs, and opened up a universe of possibilities for Hetrick and his team to explore on *Star Trek: Discovery*.

"With the level of trust and expectation we luckily have, because we've worked with these producers before, I would say we have been given a much wider range than [*TNG*-era make-up designer] Michael Westmore was," agrees

02

Hetrick. "We all know what canon looks like, and we don't want things to look completely different, but the producers didn't saddle us with all those preconceived notions at the beginning. They also didn't say, 'Have at it, do whatever you want!' No production does that.

"In general, we're following what executive producer Bryan Fuller coined as the 'evolutionary imperative,'" adds Hetrick. "Everything we're doing on the show is to reimagine the different alien species."

01 A Klingon battle helmet.

02 Glenn Hetrick applies Kor's Klingon prosthetics to actor Kenneth Mitchell.

Some of those aliens will look more familiar than others, but Hetrick insists they all bear the hallmark of their predecessors. "Everyone is aware of where we are in this timeline, but we're also trying to bring a new level of perfection to an episodic television series, and part of that is redesigning some of these characters," Hetrick explains. "When you look at the Klingon armor, for example, they're riddled with little details that are clues to even deeper references to canon.

"One of my main sticking points was that, as much as I love canon, it kind of bothered me a little bit that the Klingon wardrobe was always the same, so that's something we discussed a lot," he continues. "I really wanted to find a way to communicate to the fans that, as a species, the Klingons are far more advanced than that. All of this technology was used to reimagine the prototypical Klingon."

TECHNOLOGICAL MARVELS

Working alongside designer Neville Page and the *Discovery* showrunners, Hetrick puts a strong emphasis on collaboration, and especially values

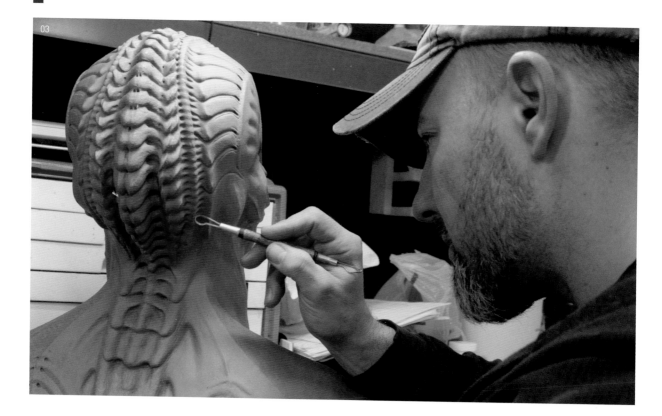

Alchemy's partnerships with other companies working at the cutting edge of 3D design. The Klingon space armor worn by the Torchbearer was one of the first things that Alchemy created for *Discovery*, and the design was entirely dependent on the use of these 3D technologies.

"We enjoy a specific and advantageous relationship with 3D Systems and Gentle Giant on this show," Hetrick tells us. Indeed, both companies are 3D-printing heavyweights: 3D Systems was co-founded by the inventor of Stereolithography (3D-printing), Charles Hull; while Gentle Giant has a worldwide reputation for turning 3D scans of movie characters into high-end collectibles. "They're allowing us to prove out concepts in terms of how the newest, biggest printers, and the toughest materials, can be utilized, whether that's for specialty costumes, special prop building, or special make-up effects," Hetrick continues.

Discovery has been more than a full time job for Hetrick and co. since they joined the production, back in 2016, and the workload has been varied and complex.

"There's been almost nothing but seven-day weeks for Neville and I, because we're so committed to this show, and we've been on it for over a year," says Hetrick. "A lot of those weeks are 80-something hours, because it's not just what you're doing in the shop; it's also the emails, and communication, and the design work."

Thankfully, the working relationship

between Hetrick and Neville Page is both well established and synergetic, helping them to navigate the rigors of a tight production schedule when developing alien ideas. Key to the efficiency with which they work is another piece of cutting edge technology, a digital sculpting tool called ZBrush, which allows the artists to sculpt and paint incredibly detailed concept models as if they were sketching on paper.

"Neville has been incredibly helpful, and ZBrush is an incredibly powerful tool in solving the problem of how to get that range of design," Hetrick explains. "We pitch ideas verbally; we'll talk to each other, and I'll say, 'Here's what I want, and here's what he wants.' And when we're talking to producers, they have ideas that they want, so we do that verbally. And then Neville, very quickly and with great efficiency, comes up with little thumbnail sketches. There was a lot of that before we started production, just in terms of aliens that didn't exist, Saru and other characters coming your way that people haven't seen before, and we really did have carte blanche to throw out all kinds of ideas."

The production would pick the three or four designs they liked best, and Neville and Hetrick would develop those further, including the sculpting of physical maquettes.

"We would get down to the one we liked best, and do that one in sculpture to a certain point, then show it to the producers and say, 'Here's what it would

03 A member of Hetrick's team refines the spine detailing on a Klingon maquette.

04 An actor is fitted with the impressive Torchbearer armor.

05 A fully painted Klingon battle helmet.

look like on the person's head,'" says Hetrick, describing the process that would lead to a finished design. "They would comment on the sculpture, then we would get the prosthetic pieces made and send them pictures with the base tone, and say, 'Let's try this paint technique; should we go a little darker? Where should we add a pattern, or make it a little lighter?'

"Early on, there was a lot more time to do that, but that's how we got into our rhythm, so today, a year-plus later, there is now a shorthand between us and the producers," Hetrick continues. "We know what our goals are, and what we're trying to achieve, so Neville and I will discuss things and he'll come up with some digital designs. Once they approve them, we'll take those digital designs and do a small-scale 3D print, and then we just go as fast as possible from that point on. We still do all our make-ups traditionally, so there's a sculpture based on that approved digital design, and we'll mold it and get the prosthetic pieces out, and generally show them to the producers with a color option or two."

GET THE KLINGON LOOK

The biggest alien presence in the new series is the Klingons, which in this incarnation display a wide variety of different looks. The rationale for this variation is that Klingons come from different clans, or "houses," that hail from different planets and environments across the Klingon Empire, which informs their physical appearances in a number of ways.

As Hetrick explains, "One of the things I said was, 'Listen, the Klingon species lives within an entire *empire*, so it's not just one planet but many, and the Klingon homeworld, Qo'noS, is only home to certain houses; why couldn't there be different houses living on different planets?' I felt that if you looked at the modern age through the lens of humanity, depending on which continent or city you're from, and the difference in architecture, food, clothing, music, art – everything would be amplified exponentially if you had a species living on an entire *empire* of planets. Bringing what I call the 'cultural patina' to all of those Klingon houses, and making each of them unique with its own internal backstory, meant every decision we made about Klingon design had a driving impetus."

"All of this technology was used to reimagine the prototypical Klingon."

Hetrick gives an example of what this might mean, saying, "For example, let's say that one of the houses was comprised of 'beast masters.' If you have to master animals, how do Klingons do it? They probably throw you in the pens with the dogs as a child, and you survive or you don't. The ones that do are going to have some pretty significant scarring all over their bodies. The reason I thought that was super cool was there are actually several references to Klingons having these incredibly powerful beasts throughout the canon. You see it with Christopher Lloyd, in *Star Trek III*, with what looks

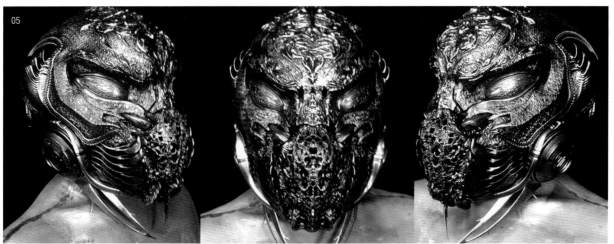

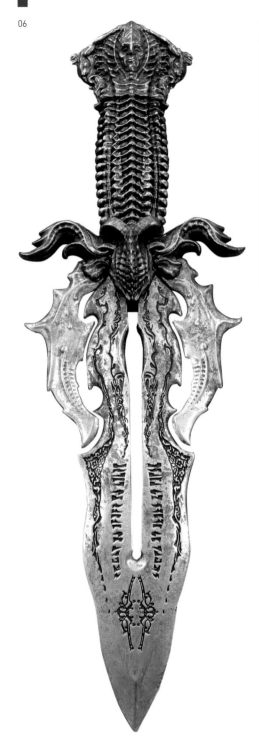

07

"The Klingons are aesthetes, they're very intelligent and highly evolved, and you can see the level of artistic integrity that certain houses have in their ships and their costumes."

like a skinned dog sitting next to him at his command chair. And later, in *The Undiscovered Country*, you see these bull mastiffs outside the gates of the snowy prison, so I wanted to grab that idea and say, 'Which Klingons would have that kind of hunter culture, where they have dogs or maybe the equivalent of a hawk, and how would that affect the way they look?'

"So that's what we were doing during the first few months of development," Hetrick continues. "Working on the process of how to take this incredible digital technology we had, and amplify it into something we thought would look completely and truly alien and futuristic, which was not accomplishable by any other standard means. And then we had to nail that Klingon aesthetic, and how it related to those make-ups, because we have a lot of them, and they're very important to the story. They're not just a foil or the enemy; they're probably my favorite part of the *Star Trek* universe, so it was important to get it right."

Hetrick was also determined that the eventual look of the Klingons intimated a greater degree of complexity within their culture than previously seen. "The Klingons are aesthetes, they're very intelligent and highly evolved, and you can see the level of artistic integrity that certain houses have in their ships and their costumes," he says. "When you look at them, they don't actually look *that* different. They're bald and they don't have hair, but you still see the traditional ridges and a lot of the traditional forms, but described in a much more complex way. And then there is all the layered sophistication of their art and culture, which makes them

infinitely more interesting from our point of view, and we hope that fans feel that way too. We're just trying to play in that space, and make the make-ups and the characters wearing make-ups as interesting and intriguing, and as rich, as their human counterparts that we love so much."

STYLING SARU

Aside from the new Klingons, one of the standout characters has been Lt. Saru, the *Discovery*'s Kelpien first officer, played by fan-favorite creature performer Doug Jones.

"That character went through two completely different phases of development," notes Hetrick. "We built something and put it on Doug, and after getting input from different people, we said, 'Let's look at another version.' So we built that and got it approved, but the initial look was done in the good old days of pre-production, before we started shooting, so we had a bit more time.

"When we finally locked on to the final look for Saru, we only had a very short turnaround, so it became more indicative of what we're doing with every character now," he adds. "Having already built and looked at one thing, we were saying, 'No, it's something different!' From the amount of time we had between Neville's designs to a physical version of that design on set, it was probably only three weeks."

It may take time to populate the *Star Trek: Discovery* universe with alien inhabitants, but Alchemy have no shortage of new characters waiting in the wings for their moment on camera.

"We've already come so far with

08

09

certain ideas, and fallen passionately in love with them," Hetrick admits, "but we got to the point where we realized it wasn't going to happen this season, either because it's impractical or maybe that character need has gone away. We were talking about some really huge things that ended up not finding their way into the season, but we're definitely not done with those. They're just on the back burner, because we're waiting for them to say to us, 'Do you guys have any ideas for this ship in Season 2?' Oh boy, do we! We will continue to champion the things that we've fallen in love with.

"There are probably a solid 10 to 12 things I would be amazed if we didn't eventually find a way to get in there," Hetrick continues, "because Neville and I are so passionate about certain concepts, whether they're things we've seen in high fashion, medical technology, or even engineering technology, that use 3D printing techniques that are un-accomplishable any other way, and are being used in other fields right now. Maybe we can use one as a piece of armor, or maybe we're looking at the insides of something, or it could be a bioluminescent application; there's a whole group of ideas that we came up with during our research on the first season, and neither Neville nor I are going to let them go, even if it takes us until Season 5 to do them!"

Hetrick is well aware of the resistance some corners of *Star Trek* fandom had towards the new series before it began airing, but he hopes they're at least giving *Discovery* a try.

"I saw a lot of negativity to the leaked material, and the trailers that were released," Hetrick concedes, "but when we did the big *Star Trek* convention

in Las Vegas in the summer, it began going the other way. As a *Star Trek* fan, I can understand that, because it took me a long time to come to *The Next Generation*, and accept the idea that there could be a new and amazing addition to Gene Roddenberry's universe, so I know where they're coming from. I just hope everybody at least watches it, so they can see what we're talking about. After we talked about the show in Vegas, people started going through social media to see all of those ideas, how nuanced the design of the Klingon species is, and how much reverence there was for *Star Trek* canon, so I think the tide is starting to turn."

With *Star Trek: Discovery* now confirmed as returning for a second season, Glenn Hetrick is pleased with the work his team at Alchemy Studios did on Season 1, and how it fits into a rich tradition of make-up FX for the franchise.

"*Star Trek: The Next Generation* especially was famous for doing these huge, two-part season finale/season opener episodes, and I think our first two episodes have that epic quality," says Hetrick. "I think they're going to bring in new fans. When you watch those first two episodes, you're seeing a two-hour event that is just amazing, and the show will only get more amazing!" ⋆

06 The ornate detailing of this Klingon blade was made possible by 3D printing techniques.

07 Klingon masks in various states of completion.

08 T'Kuvma (Chris Obi).

09 Glenn Hetrick shows prototypes for L'Rell's make-up.

L'RELL

MARY CHIEFFO

For a Klingon warrior, Mary Chieffo is surely far too approachable. And great company as well. Bursting with friendly enthusiasm, the actor couldn't conceal her excitement over her role as L'Rell in *Star Trek: Discovery*, spilling the raktajino beans about her character to *Star Trek Magazine* one sunny morning in Las Vegas.

Words: Ian Spelling

"This whole time has been amazing. A-maze-ing," Mary Chieffo raves, speaking backstage at the Rio Suites Hotel, towards the end of *Star Trek Las Vegas 2017*. "I've been here the whole time, and the fans are so passionate. I've loved meeting everyone, and hearing their excitement about *Star Trek: Discovery*. I've already seen fans in *Discovery* uniforms, which is crazy, since we're not even on the air yet."

Chieffo has thrown herself into the fun of the convention, to the extent that she was one of the judges for the event's costume contest. "I met Robert O'Reilly!" she enthuses (O'Reilly played the Klingon Gowron in numerous *Next Generation* and *Deep Space Nine* episodes). "I am just so excited to be a part of this. All of it."

> "Bryan [Fuller] saw me as this six-foot-tall, angular-featured woman, and said, 'I think we should base this design kind of on you.'"
>
> MARY CHIEFFO

Chieffo, who plays L'Rell, a Klingon battle deck commander in *Star Trek: Discovery*, had already spent nearly a week in Las Vegas, immersing herself in the world's biggest annual gathering of *Star Trek* fans. On the morning of her first full day there, the actor – a stage veteran from her time at the legendary Juilliard School of performing arts, but a fresh face to television viewers – had simply blended in, roaming around just like any other regular fan, unnoticed, observing. A few hours later, and that all changed when she took to the stage alongside co-stars Kenneth Mitchell, Sam Vartholomeos, and Wilson Cruz, as the actors participated in a *Discovery* panel to a packed auditorium. For the rest of the weekend, Chieffo took *Star Trek Las Vegas* by the horns, interacting with fans, assuring them that *Discovery*'s Klingons will be well served, signing autographs, and posing for photographs with anyone who asked.

Right in the middle of Chieffo's *Star Trek Las Vegas* experience, she joined *Star Trek Magazine* for breakfast at one of the Rio's restaurants. For the better part of an hour, she introduced us – passionately, enthusiastically, and proudly – to L'Rell. She even spoke some Klingon, although her guttural phrases are hard to replicate in print. And despite us being nestled in a corner booth at a far end of the restaurant, a few fans still recognized Chieffo. How could they not? She's a striking woman, standing at six-feet-tall. As one might expect, the fans maintained a polite distance until after the interview concluded.

"I've always been a sci-fi and fantasy fan. I grew up with that whole genre, loving it, but I didn't get introduced to

Star Trek until the reboot movies," admits Chieffo, who pronounces her name Chief-oh. "From that, I just fell in love with the chemistry of the characters, and all of the great tenets we love about the franchise. That motivated me to go back, and I watched all of the original-cast movies."

As is so often the case, *Star Trek* brings generations together, and Chieffo's family was no exception. "Once my dad saw I loved it, he was like, 'Oh, well we got to watch the originals,'" she laughs.

Having already gained an appreciation for the series, being cast in *Discovery* gave Chieffo an excuse to watch even more. "Once I got this role, I did go back and watch all the Klingon-featured episodes, from every series," she says. "So, in the past year, I've fallen in love with every Klingon character, from every different iteration."

MOLD MAKER

Chieffo, who hails from New York City, and is the daughter of actors Beth Grant and Michael Chieffo, recalls that she arrived at her *Discovery* audition raring to go, with a reasonably good grasp of Klingon culture. She was subsequently floored and flattered by a comment from Bryan Fuller, who co-created *Discovery*.

"Bryan saw me as this six-foot-tall, angular-featured woman, and said, 'I think we should base this design kind of on you,'" Chieffo smiles. "So, initially, I came onto the show because of my build, which is so thrilling, because coming out of school being six-foot-tall, and being unique in various ways, it's hard to put me in a mold. But then to have a creature, an alien, that fits so much of what I can fill, with my relationship with language, and having performed Shakespeare, it was perfect, they knew what I was capable of."

By now, fans will have seen a few episodes of *Discovery*, and are familiar with both the show's central characters and basic set-up – it's set 10 years before the Kirk-Spock era, and focuses on a nascent war between the Federation and the Klingon Empire. Chieffo stresses that *Discovery* picks up threads from the original *Star Trek* series and its follow-ups while, at the same time, being very much a *Trek* show in its own right.

"I think it really does do both," the actor notes. "I keep saying, I think the power of love is something that seems very clichéd, but it's something that has always been innate in the franchise. Our ability to see 'the other' and to see ourselves in the other – that's a huge, huge theme that goes across the board, in every iteration of the franchise, and we have that in spades in *Discovery*. And you see it on both sides, which I think is one of the fresher aspects, maybe, within the Klingons and within the Federation. Characters are struggling, and having internal struggles. Then, in a more symbolic way, you see Sonequa playing Michael Burnham, our protagonist, and you see her as a woman of color, representing that.

"As the actors, I think we're very aware of what we're doing with L'Rell, and her being a commander," Chieffo continues. "I definitely feel that there are all these symbols, and new ways of representing our gender, our race, whatever it is. I don't have big speeches where I'm like, 'I am a female Klingon, and I have struggles.' It's more that we are there and present, and we're aware that there will be that little girl or boy who can see that male or female character, and we will resonate with them."

01

02

01 L'Rell (Mary Chieffo) meets with T'Kuvma (Chris Obi), the Klingon leader.

02 Mary Chieffo onstage with Kenneth Mitchell (Kol), at *Star Trek Las Vegas 2017*.

THE WEAVERS OF LIES

When we ask Chieffo what it is that really jazzes her about L'Rell, she smiles almost as broadly as she is tall, and recounts gushing to *Discovery*'s writers and producers about how she'd never imagined that L'Rell could have so many facets to explore.

As the Klingon commander, Chieffo says she gets to be a "tomboy, and gross, and fierce, and scary," but that the character also reveals a deep capacity for love and compassion. This all fits in with *Discovery*'s nuanced depiction of Klingon culture.

"The official backstory is that you meet L'Rell as T'Kuvma's battle deck commander, which in layman's terms means she is his chief strategist. I'm kind of his campaign manager," she jokes. "For the beginning half of my journey, you really see me as someone who is doing a lot of work behind the scenes, watching T'Kuvma, and making sure he's staying on topic. T'Kuvma is the leader of House T'Kuvma, so it's me letting him do his job. Now, what's fun is that we later reveal that while I'm House T'Kuvma, my mother's side was House *Mokai*, which is a matriarchal Klingon house of spies.

"They are known as the watcher clan, the deceivers, the weavers of lies," Chieffo continues, with a glint in her eye. "They work in the shadows. I think that's a very interesting quality for a Klingon, that L'Rell actually does not crave the mantle of leadership. She wants to get things done, but she knows how to be a team player. I always joke that L'Rell would love to execute plan A, B, or C,

but she usually has to resort to plan X, Y, or Z. She understands that that's part of life and the world. There's one phrase that I say that is like her tenet," Chieffo then utters something in fluent Klingon, "which means, 'use compromise to conquer.' Getting to see her adherence to that, but also her struggle with what it really means, is so interesting."

Chieffo goes on to share that there are L'Rell scenes in one episode that show just how devious her character can be. Fearful of revealing spoilers, she asks when this issue of *Star Trek Magazine* will be out, and Chieffo's eyes light up once she's told the episode in question will have already aired.

"OK, then perfect!" Chieffo grins, happy to spread some Klingon gossip. "Episode four, for sure, you get to see Klingon flirting."

The scenes happen in "The Butcher's Knife Cares Not for the Lamb's Cry," directed by Olatunde Osunsanmi, and written by Jesse Alexander and Aron Eli Coleite.

"What was beautiful about episode four was that it's such a great example of the collaborative process," says Chieffo. "From what I'd been doing in episodes one and two, [the writers] were like, 'Oh, let's see how we can create this story.' They gave me that opportunity. They wrote these great scenes, and from that we found a nuance, and an excitement. There's also a real sensitivity and heart. You get to see the sensuality. I want to say something more specific, because I'm so used to not being able to talk about things," Chieffo grimaces.

L'RELL

BATTLE DECK COMMANDER, HOUSE OF T'KUVMA

As war rages between the Klingon Empire and the Federation, L'Rell remains determined to support the leader of her house, T'Kuvma, who seeks to unite the Klingon houses following generations of disarray within the Empire.

A respected strategist, her unique white armor marks L'Rell out as a powerful figure in T'Kuvma's crew, to be feared as much as she is venerated.

And with good reason, as L'Rell belongs to two of the Great Houses of the Empire. A warrior of the House of T'Kuvma, L'Rell's mother was of the House Mokai, the Klingon house of spies, often referred to as "the weavers of lies." L'Rell's affiliation with both houses creates personal conflict for the commander, echoed in the way she is viewed by her enemies, both in the Federation and within the Empire itself.

"I will say that the last scene in episode four is very telling for L'Rell, because you see that, even though she does things that might seem evil or mean in the moment, ultimately her heart is in the right place," Chieffo adds. "Her heart wins out, despite her better judgment, and she really does care about her fellow Klingons, and upholding T'Kuvma's message about being unified as 24 houses. She'll do everything in her power to make his message reach everyone. She leads with her heart, but doesn't let her heart get in the way of what she needs to do for the cause. She's willing to sacrifice things she loves for the cause, because she loves the cause. There's something much larger than herself at stake, and she is willing to do what she needs to do."

03 Mary Chieffo at *Star Trek Las Vegas 2017.*

04 *Discovery*'s Klingons howl during a death ritual.

A JOB ON TOP OF A JOB

Beyond the character's, well... character, there are other major components of L'Rell to consider and address. Case in point: the make-up and prosthetics. Anyone who's read interviews with *Star Trek* regulars who've played aliens, like Michael Dorn (Worf), Rene Auberjonois (Odo), Armin Shimerman (Quark), or John Billingsley (Phlox), has heard the horror stories of hours spent in a make-up chair, having their prosthetics carefully applied and, after a long day of shooting, even more carefully removed. They were the first ones at the studio in the morning, and the last ones to leave at night. It was a job on top of a job. On the other hand, as several of them have cited, it served the dual purpose of allowing them time to become lost in their respective

characters and, even better, provided a measure of public anonymity.

"Well, I do joke that I have a weird, masochistic sensibility, because I love a giant challenge," Chieffo says, laughing. "I love the challenge of the language; I love the challenge of the prosthetics. Sure, there are long days and hours where I get tired, but there's something about getting up in the morning and getting into that chair. And we have a system now. We blast '80s music in the morning. I love the incredible artists in the prosthetics trailer. James MacKinnon is our head. He worked on *Deep Space Nine* (and on the 2009 *Star Trek* feature). He's been around forever, and he's so meticulous. That whole process is now very fun, and it also helps me to take two hours of my day where I'm not freaking out over my lines."

When it comes to seeing herself in the mirror, in full make-up and costume, Chieffo isn't phased, which she puts down to her training at Juilliard.

"I did a lot of mask and movement work in college," she tells us. "That was always something I really gravitated towards, and really loved. This caters to that so perfectly. I literally have a different face, and a different shape to my head. I found with L'Rell that I have this beautiful back of my head, that's kind of an arc." Chieffo reaches a hand behind her head to illustrate. "She has all these sensors back there, and I just started to develop this head tilt upon looking at myself. Talking to Neville Page, our designer, he said, 'That completely makes sense, because you really do almost have stronger senses in the back of your head.' You get to push the limits of expression. You get to use your eyes as the window to the soul."

And let's not forget about the Klingon language, as much of the Klingon dialogue will be spoken by the actors in Klingon, with viewers at home reading English subtitles at the bottom of their screens.

"As far as speaking Klingon, I keep making the Shakespeare analogy, in that we want to get it right. You have to get it right," says Chieffo, not the first Klingon to mention the Bard. "We're all taking that very seriously, and are working with [Klingon language translator] Robyn Stewart. There have been a few really amazing moments on set, where the crew doesn't speak Klingon but they're watching the scene, and they get what's going on. There was one where the Director of Photography was like, 'Oh, yeah, that part where you go over and protect him…' And that's exactly what I was doing. It really helps you realize the importance of what happens between the lines."

05 Mary Chieffo meets some fellow Klingons at *Star Trek Las Vegas.*

06 Mary Chieffo as L'Rell.

Chieffo is clearly downright giddy about seeing L'Rell emerge as part of the *Discovery* marketing and merchandising juggernaut. The day before this interview, she'd tweeted a picture of herself standing beneath her L'Rell teaser poster in the rotunda at *Star Trek Las Vegas.* She was still psyched about that moment, but looking forward to wrapping her hands around something even more tangible.

"It was thrilling to see the poster, to see this giant L'Rell eye," Chieffo notes with enthusiasm, "but I am really excited about the idea of an action figure, particularly because so much thought and effort was put into her armor, and the fact that she isn't overly sexualized. Kids can play with her, and be like, 'I'm L'Rell. I'm badass.' Hopefully they won't say that if they're eight! But to think of kids being able to start to understand that armor is armor, through an action figure, and understand that in that moment she kicks butt, but it doesn't have anything to do with her gender."

As Mary Chieffo disappears to spread the L'Rell love around the exhibition halls of *Star Trek Las Vegas,* we can only wish her success. Or should we say, Qapla'! ⚮

STAR TREK
DISCOVERY

KENNETH MITCHELL

KOL

If there is one Klingon in *Star Trek: Discovery* who seems closest to those seen in the original *Star Trek*, then it's the devious Kol. Cunning, fearless, and determined to crush the Federation, Kol is all warrior. *Star Trek Magazine* speaks to actor Kenneth Mitchell about finding his place in the pantheon of *Star Trek* villains.

Words: Ian Spelling

There's no quick-start guide or instruction manual for actors auditioning to portray a Klingon. Nor, as Kenneth Mitchell notes, is there a barometer as to why one actor might be selected over another for a role like Kol.

"I don't know what they were thinking, actually," Mitchell recalls. "I was working in Vancouver at the time, on another television series, so I couldn't go into the room to do the audition. I had put myself on tape, which I did in my hotel room. I submitted that tape to the casting directors in LA, and I guess that [*Discovery*'s co-creator and executive producer] Bryan Fuller and his team, [executive producers and showrunners] Gretchen Berg and Aaron Harberts, thankfully saw something in me. They asked me to come and re-test for the part, so they flew me back to LA and I read for them, in person."

Even then, the audition wasn't a run-of-the-mill experience for Mitchell.

It transpires that it wasn't only *Star Trek* fans who were kept in the dark during the casting process – the actors involved were up against a veil of subterfuge as well.

"During that audition, everything was changed – the names of everything, the characters, everyone," the actor confides. "I knew I was auditioning for *Star Trek*, but they were even secretive about that. That being said, I was super-excited about it, and my audition piece was actually one of T'Kuvma's speeches from the pilot. There was another scene, too. I remember reading it for the first time in front of Bryan, Gretchen, and Aaron, and they were... You could see they were interested, but they were also a little bit confused, because I was saying the wrong names. I was naming things that had been changed from the script.

"They weren't aware that the casting directors had changed some of the names on the audition scripts, for security purposes," Mitchell laughs. "I

was supposed to say, 'Remain Klingon,' but I was saying something completely different. Bryan was like, 'You know you're a Klingon, right?' I'm silent, but in my head I'm like, 'Holy s...! What is going on?' Then, he took it upon himself to explain further as to the direction of the series, and how they really wanted to explore the Klingon world beyond what had been done before. I was really fascinated by it. I read the scene a couple times again, and I was hired on my way home in the cab."

CONNECTING WITH KOL

As viewers know by now, Kol is the leader of the House of Kor, one of the 24 Klingon houses. He's a fierce warrior, who clashes not only with the Federation but also he's far from being on the same page as the instigator of the war – the religious crusader and Klingon leader, T'Kuvma (Chris Obi).

02

COMMANDER KOL

A proud warrior of the House of Kor, Commander Kol takes up T'Kuvma's quest to unify the Klingons, but only to quench his thirst for power.

One of the Great Houses of the Klingon Empire, the House of Kor is a powerful and respected voice among the Empire's 24 most prominent houses. Led by respected military leader Kor, son of Rynar, the royal blood of the Klingon Imperial family burns fiercely in the veins of its warriors.

Kol regards the honor of his family to come above all else, and would sooner die than live with a mark on the name of his ancestral lineage. The family is everything, and every member is responsible for the actions of their kin. But Kol is also ambitious, and embraces the opportunities offered to him by the war with the Federation. Kol may be proud of his heritage, a defender of the house of Kor, but for him it's all about the honor and power of Kol.

> "They really wanted to explore the Klingon world beyond what had been done before. I was really fascinated by it."

"Kol has these disagreements and conflicts with T'Kuvma and his house, and it kind of launches that relationship throughout the rest of the season," Mitchell explains, choosing his words carefully to avoid spoiler territory. "Kol is on a bit of a path to power, and he also wants to protect his people, not only amongst the Klingon houses, but against the Federation."

Not surprisingly, Mitchell notes, his Klingon costume and prosthetics are "heavy and hot," and they provide their share of impediments and challenges. Upping the ante when it comes to delivering his performance as Kol is the fact that Mitchell and his fellow actors speak in the Klingon tongue, with fans at home reading English translations of the dialogue on their screens. Mitchell gives full credit to *Discovery*'s Klingon dialect coach, Rea Nolan, as the person he thanks for helping him maintain his sanity while

trying to speak Klingon, take after take, hour after hour, day after day.

"When we do the work, we have Rea on set," Mitchell says. "She's like our right arm. She's our mother, she's our psychiatrist. She's a massive *Star Trek* fan, and she's the one coming up to us between takes, exuding excitement and also coming up and giving us notes. In-between the takes, it'll be like, 'Yeah, you need to really highlight this Klingon sound, or that sound.' It becomes very specific. The reason it becomes *so* specific is because we want to get it right for that one percent of the fans that actually know the language. They're just as important, if not more important, than everyone else.

"It's an incredibly challenging and complex language. It's complicated for a reason, so that it feels alien-like," Mitchell adds. "It takes a lot of muscle memory to memorize every separate syllable. My kids and my family think I'm crazy, but at the end of the day, it is all worth it. It adds such an amazing texture to the show, and is a real asset to helping the audience learn more about the Klingon culture."

With *Discovery*'s emphasis on creating a believably alien society for the Klingons, did learning a new language make it difficult to portray Kol as a fully-defined character, and deliver a performance with the required emotional resonance?

prosthetics and speaking Klingon – it's physically challenging, and it's mentally challenging – but what keeps me going is everyone's dedication. It's the passion for the franchise and for this series.

"So, I'm constantly having to remind myself of that when I want to rip off my prosthetics, or I'm overheating, or whatever the case may be, or I'm pacing back and forth for two weeks trying to learn my Klingon dialogue," he adds. "It's daunting, but at the end of the day it always comes back to, 'You know what? You are part of something magical. You are part of something special, so just keep going. Keep going. It's all worth it.'"

As the conversation draws to a close, we point out to Mitchell that *Star Trek* shows tend to run for a long time. Thus, and depending on the fallout of *Discovery*'s explosive mid-season finale, he could end up sporting Klingon prosthetics for perhaps another seven years. Mitchell sounds prepared, even stoked, at such a prospect.

"I'm ready as ever," says Mitchell. "The big thing for me, the beauty of it is, I like working, but I *love* to be on a project that I love. And *Discovery* is a project I love. This is a marrying of the two, hopefully. I would love to be on a show that has longevity, but ideally if you're going to be on a show for a long time, you want it to be a show that you love, and I've got a feeling that this is it." ★

"You just want to come in and get it right," Mitchell reflects. "You don't always, and the producers and directors sometimes say, 'Well, it wasn't perfect, but what's most important is the emotion behind it, and the story that we're telling.' And that's completely true. The goal is to marry both of them. You want to get the dialogue right, and you want to get the essence of the scene right. You don't always come away from a scene with it being perfect, but you can fix a few things here and there in post [during the ADR process, where dialogue is re-recorded in a sound studio for various reasons] – but at the end of the day you just want to do the best job you can on the set so that you need to do as little as possible in post."

GOING GREEN

Prior to taking on the role of the devious Kol, Mitchell had been a regular face in genre television, with guest star or recurring roles in shows like *Odyssey 5*, *Jericho*, *Flashpoint*, *Grimm*, *Minority Report*, and *Frequency*. With a résumé filled with sci-fi, horror, and fantasy projects, Mitchell's longstanding familiarity with, and understanding of, how such effects-heavy productions are made held him in good stead as he ventured into the *Star Trek* franchise.

"Every experience is helpful for the next one," Mitchell notes. "And, in terms of these kinds of experiences, a specific example would be the idea of working with a green screen. It's no mystery that in *Discovery* we have to use

> ## "I feel really blessed to be on the show, and also to be working with the people involved."

a lot of green screen. So, a lot of times you're just staring out into the green, but you're having to imagine there's a planet or there's another ship there. That this is happening right in front of you.

"Those can be challenges as an actor," Mitchell continues, "but when you have these other experiences from shows that you've done before, you start to build up a certain technique, or a better understanding of how things are executed, how they'll edit together, and how'll they look on screen."

SOMETHING MAGICAL

According to Mitchell "it means everything" to him to become a part of the *Star Trek* universe, and its 50-plus-year history. As an actor, he explains, it's a special moment whenever you become a part of something iconic.

"I feel really blessed to be on the show, and also to be working with the people involved," Mitchell says. "And then there's this sense of responsibility to the fans, and this whole, amazing, beautiful, magical community that's out there. It's not an easy job, being in the

01 Commander Kol, as played by Kenneth Mitchell.

02 Mitchell on stage at *Star Trek Las Vegas 2017*.

03 Kol (Mitchell) aboard the Klingon Ship of the Dead.

CREW MANIFEST

KENNETH MITCHELL

Canadian-born Kenneth Mitchell didn't initially set out to become an actor, graduating from university with a degree in Landscape Architecture. It was during his time working at Kilcoo Camp in Ontario that he caught the performing bug, going on to appear in a number of short films before scoring his first part in a major television production, as Spencer Matthew in the drama series *Leap Years*. Prior to playing Kol in *Star Trek: Discovery*, Mitchell was best known for his recurring role as Eric Green in the post-apocalyptic sci-fi series *Jericho*, and as Sam Lucas in 15 episodes of supernatural chiller *Ghost Whisperer*.

STAR TREK
DISCOVERY

A LIFE LESS ORDINARY

His appearances on the show may have been brief, but Sam Vartholomeos' life has already been changed by *Star Trek: Discovery*. The actor behind the *U.S.S. Shenzhou*'s Ensign Danby Connor is fully cognizant of how appearing on the show has impacted his day-to-day existence, with fans welcoming him with open arms into the *Star Trek* family and eager to see him at conventions for years to come. He even found the infamous "technobabble" instructive – after a fashion.

Words: Ian Spelling

tar Trek actors long before Sam Vartholomeos and long after Sam Vartholomeos have bemoaned and will bemoan what *Star Trek* actors call "technobabble" – that nearly impenetrable, hard-to-remember, even-harder-to-deliver scientific and/or medical dialogue that's fairly unique to the franchise. So, what's the most ridiculous thing Vartholomeos has had to say as Ensign Danby Connor on *Star Trek: Discovery*, and how badly did that scene go?

A smile crosses the young actor's face as he contemplates the question. The answer, he notes, wasn't a line that he uttered, but rather it was spoken to Ensign Connor by Michelle Yeoh as Captain Georgiou. "Well, one thing I'll say is there was a line that Michelle had where she was telling me to do something," Vartholomeos recalls. "And she said, 'Not an attosecond later.'"

A *what* second later?

"Exactly," Vartholomeos says, nodding. "An attosecond."

A-T-O?

"An A-T-T-O second."

OK, then.

"Do you know what an attosecond is?" Vartholomeos asks aloud.

Not a darn clue.

"An attosecond is one quintillionth of a second," he explains. "I think it is, if I'm saying this correctly, what a second is to 37 million years, or something like that."

Wow.

"Yeah, so Michelle said that to me and I was looking at the script," Vartholomeos continues. "I said, 'What is an attosecond?' I looked it up and that helps with making it real, actually. There was this other line too... Oh, I can't remember it now, but I swear I'm going to take it with me to the grave."

Actually, no, he won't.

"I can't even remember it, I know!" Vartholomeos admits, laughing. "I'm a liar. I was caught red-handed. Oh, if I remember it, I'll tell you."

IN IT FOR LIFE

Vartholomeos, at the time of this interview, is at *Star Trek Las Vegas*. It's his first-ever *Trek* convention, following a quick appearance at San Diego Comic-Con a few weeks earlier, and during it he meets countless fans, immerses himself in the world of *Trek*, and shakes hands with actors from earlier *Trek* shows and movies. Among the many useful takeaways from his time at *Star Trek Las Vegas* is a lesson in what it means to become a part of the *Star Trek* universe. That's to say, once you're in one episode...

"You're in it for life," Vartholomeos notes, finishing the sentence. "I already have fans telling me now, 'Come back next year, and come back the year after…'"

"I think it will be a part of my life from now on, and being a 22-year-old guy, I have the rest of my life to be part of *Star Trek*, and that means a lot to me," he says. "I have a great responsibility now,

"We have an infinite amount of possibilities for where this show can go while upholding the history of *Star Trek*."

01

The Lives of Danby Connor

As operations officer aboard the *U.S.S. Shenzhou*, Ensign Danby Connor was an integral part of the ship's crew, forging a friendly comradeship with fellow bridge officers Michael Burnham, Saru, and Keyla Detmer. When Burnham went on an EVA to investigate an unknown object in an uninhabited binary star system, it was Connor who was her point of contact back on the bridge, and who kept an eye on her radiation levels. ("The Vulcan Hello")

After Burnham was relieved of duty and sent to the brig, Connor was injured when, during the Klingon attack on the *Shenzhou* and the Federation fleet, his console exploded. Asked by Captain Georgiou if he could make it to sickbay unaided, he responded that he could, but en route became confused and wound up in the brig, where, before a horrified Burnham's eyes, he was sucked into space when the bulkhead exploded. ("Battle at the Binary Stars") Later, when the crew of the *U.S.S. Discovery* found themselves in the Mirror Universe, Burnham came face to face with a malevolent Mirror Danby Connor, who had risen to captain of the *Shenzhou*. Burnham was forced to kill the Mirror Connor when he attacked her in a turbolift. ("Despite Yourself")

we all do, to continue this legacy, so that one day my kids can be *Star Trek* fans and their kids can be *Star Trek* fans."

Vartholomeos goes on to emphasize that *Discovery* pays tribute to the *Star Trek* shows and films that came before it. Further, he notes, it builds on what we've seen previously and then sets out on its own path. "It does absolutely pay tribute to what came before, and it's funny that it's a prequel, but with this new platform we have an infinite amount of possibilities for where this show can go while upholding the history of *Star Trek*.

"And, and one thing I can say, is that this is *Star Trek* to the core. We don't want to upset fans. We want to pay tribute to the fans of the original series and *The Next Generation*, and all those other *Star Trek* series, while creating a show that is appealing to new fans, to keep it alive."

The actor's character, Ensign Danby Connor, is the *U.S.S. Shenzhou*'s ops officer. Vartholomeos describes Connor as "*Star Trek* and Starfleet through and through," adding: "That is one thing

I really like about him. Nothing really conflicts with him. He is all about the Prime Directive, and there's a captain and there's a lieutenant commander – and everyone follows a code. When that code, and when the Prime Directive, all get crossed, his wires get crossed. He kind of uses Captain Georgiou as his North Star, and he wants to learn from her. I really wanted to make that clear about Connor: he wants to learn and move up."

MAKING IT REAL

Vartholomeos jokes that he's seen all of the *Discovery* sets, but not worked on each and every one, and he's not beamed anywhere. Turning more serious, he points out that performing on such finely detailed sets enables him to more easily slip into character and pretend to be a young man in space earning his stripes amidst a Federation/Klingon war and alongside far more experienced senior officers.

"All the sets, including the Klingon sets, they're just so amazing," Vartholomeos says. "I can't imagine

"I haven't worked with the Klingons, but I've worked with people on different ships as well, and that is really cool, because when you're on each ship you're in the world," Vartholomeos says. "You're on the ship with this one crew for however many months, however many years, and you become a family. And a family has problems, and a family has their really happy moments, and I'm really, really excited to say that it's been nothing but happy moments with the *Shenzhou* crew."

I'M GONNA LIVE FOREVER?

Vartholomeos arrived at *Discovery* with just two other major television credits to his name. He was a lead guest star in an episode of *Bull* that aired around the same time as the *Discovery* premiere, and, a few years ago, he spoke a couple of lines of dialogue in an installment of the Kevin Bacon-starring series *The Following*. So, some background would seem to be in order. Born in Queens, New York, he attended LaGuardia High School, known by many as the "Fame" school, home to many an aspiring performer and also the inspiration for both the movie *Fame* and the television show of the same name.

Right now, Vartholomeos explains, picking up the story, "I go to City College in Washington Heights [in New York City] and I'm studying psychology there, obviously while keeping up with acting. I have a coach who I work with regularly, but I wanted to study something else. I didn't want to be immersed in theater or acting. I wanted

"Danby Connor is all about the Prime Directive."

to explore different areas of myself, which I think helped with what I'm doing. But, having said that, I also like to keep myself away from the business as much as I can."

Realizing that last sentence requires a bit of clarification, Vartholomeos adds: "So, this is funny. While I was auditioning for *Discovery*, I was going to school and working from 10pm to 6am every night at the garage my dad works at. So, I was a bit of a mechanic there, and that I think helped make Sam Vartholomeos the young man he is today, not always focusing on the business – because it can really eat you alive. So, I give the business the respect it deserves, because it does deserve respect, but, at the end of the day, the scene is done, the work is done, and you can't focus on it. When the audition is done, it's done, and you did everything you could.

"And that is the most important thing, doing everything you can in the moment, especially on *Discovery*," he says. "I think every actor can say this, where you think, 'You know, I could have done more. I think I could have done more.' As soon as I got this job, even before, even in the audition, I said, 'I will never say that on the set. I will never, ever say that.' Every day is played like your last, and that has helped me tremendously." ⬩

what it's like getting to work on the Klingon sets. But, the *Shenzhou* set is amazing. The costumes are amazing. The transporter room and the brig, everything is... It's really groovy.

"It helps so much, just the complexity and just how specific everything is," he continues. "You look down in the transporter room and there's glass on the floor and you see pipes and lights and all these things that just... you're probably not even going to see on camera, but it just helps so much in making it real for us. That is one thing I wanted to do in this series, that I want to do in this series, is make it real, as real as possible, for myself, because that just helps. It's easy to think of, 'What? A transporter room? What is this?' But if you make it real, it will shine through."

Vartholomeos is happy to heap praise on his *Discovery* costars. He describes it as a "pleasure to work with everyone" in the cast, which is comprised of experienced actors such as Yeoh, Doug Jones, and Sonequa Martin-Green.

01 Fight to the death: the Mirror Universe Danby Connor attacks Michael Burnham. ("Despite Yourself")

02 Beaming aboard the *I.S.S. Shenzhou*, Lorca, Burnham, and Tyler are met by its captain, Danby Connor. ("Despite Yourself")

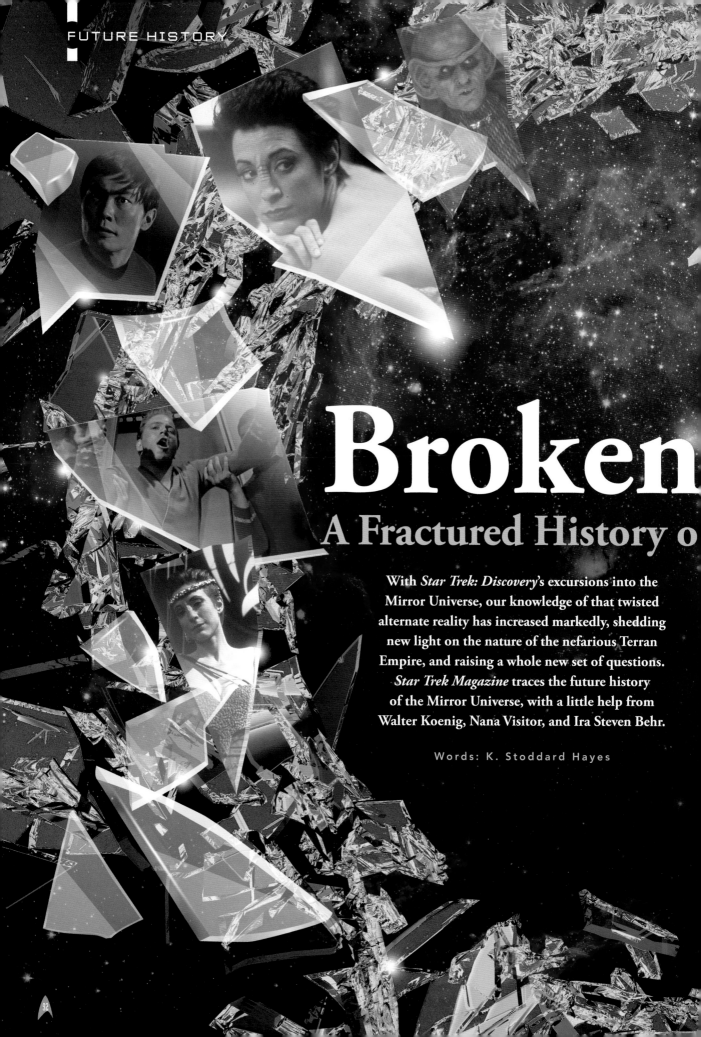

Broken

A Fractured History o

With *Star Trek: Discovery*'s excursions into the Mirror Universe, our knowledge of that twisted alternate reality has increased markedly, shedding new light on the nature of the nefarious Terran Empire, and raising a whole new set of questions. *Star Trek Magazine* traces the future history of the Mirror Universe, with a little help from Walter Koenig, Nana Visitor, and Ira Steven Behr.

Words: K. Stoddard Hayes

Mirror
he Mirror Universe

While the Federation has long known that parallel quantum universes exist, one parallel universe in particular seems to have a remarkable affinity with that of the Federation. Interactions with the so-called "Mirror Universe" are more frequent than travel to any other known dimension. And these interactions over 200 years show that the two realities are – and remain – similar in ways that seem scientifically impossible.

The Mirror Universe, after untold ages of separate evolution, ought to be very different from the Prime Universe.

And yet time after time, identical planets and sentient species, identical cultures and technologies – even identical individuals – appear at the same time in each reality.

Terran Terror

The known history of the Mirror Universe is dominated by the rise and fall of the Terran Empire. The Empire began its expansion beyond the Sol system with the capture of a Vulcan scout ship by Mirror Zefram Cochrane and his followers, in a twisted parallel of our own historic First Contact. ("In a Mirror, Darkly")

A hundred years later, the Terran Empire controls territory that probably corresponds with the heart of the Federation in the Prime Universe. Vulcans serve as loyal second class citizens under Terran rule, while other nearby races such as Andorians, Tellarites, and Denobulans have also been conquered. Other species living

01 Zefram Cochrane and co. assemble to greet the arriving Vulcans…

02 …with markedly different results, in "In a Mirror, Darkly."

03 Michael Burnham grapples with Mirror Lorca in "What's Past Is Prologue."

04 Terran Emperor Philippa Georgiou.

farther out in the galaxy, such as the Gorn and the Tholians, still pose a threat to the Empire's hegemony.

By this period, the Empire is already "…an oppressive, racist, xenophobic culture… The Terran culture appears to be predicated upon an unconditional hatred and rejection of anything and everything other." (Michael Burnham, "Despite Yourself")

And hatred is not limited to non-humans. Conspiracy and assassination are rife in all ranks of the Terran military, and presumably among political factions as well. Senior officers like Captain Forrest and Commander Archer clash lethally over command power, while their followers scheme for their own advantage – or survival. Only the Vulcan, T'Pol, seems to feel any loyalty to her human commander, although this may be as much a matter of Vulcan culture as individual morality.

The Tholian capture of the 23rd Century Prime Universe *U.S.S. Defiant*

Going Through the Looking Glass

These are all the known ways to travel between the universes.

- Interphasic rift, *U.S.S. Defiant* NCC-1764. The Tholians used a rift to reach across time as well as between dimensions. ("In a Mirror, Darkly"/"The Tholian Web")
- Spore drive jump, *Discovery* ("Despite Yourself"). With an intelligent living navigator to interface with the spores, this technology can apparently take a ship to any destination connected to the mycelial plane of existence.
- Transport during an ion storm, Mirror Lorca ("What's Past Is Prologue"); Kirk and landing party ("Mirror, Mirror").
- Wormhole disturbance, Kira and Bashir ("Crossover"). It is unknown whether the Prophets might have had a role in this crossover via their "Celestial Temple."
- Multi-dimensional transporter, "Smiley" and Sisko ("Through the Looking Glass"), plus several subsequent incursions from one side to the other during Sisko's command of Deep Space 9.

"Great men are not 'peacemakers.' Great men are conquerors!"
MIRROR JONATHAN ARCHER

08

04

and its advanced technology is a catalyst for upheaval. Although the Tholians immediately strip the vessel of all its advanced technology, when Archer and his crew hijack the ship, it still has more than enough firepower to win a last-minute Terran victory over rebel forces.

Defiant then becomes the focus of a power struggle that will shake the Empire. Archer, as the victorious captain, wants command of the new ship plus the recognition of the emperor, while his superior, Admiral Black, plans to keep both for himself. Archer assassinates Black, only to be betrayed and assassinated by his late captain's – and subsequently his own – lover, Hoshi Sato, who brings *Defiant* home to Earth and proclaims herself emperor. ("In a Mirror, Darkly, Part II")

"Equality. Freedom. Cooperation... delusions that Terrans shed millennia ago."
EMPEROR GEORGIOU

Whether Sato's coup succeeds or not is unknown. Either way, the Empire thrives and expands until, by the mid-23rd Century, it controls all of known space – or claims to. However, the rebellion of the 22nd Century has persisted, or risen again, and under the leadership of the Klingon known as "Firewolf" once again threatens the stability of the Empire.

05

Rediscovering the Empire

In 2257, the *U.S.S. Discovery* arrives in the Mirror Universe – apparently by accident – via a series of spore drive jumps. Commander Saru's skepticism about the coincidence later proves justified, when Michael Burnham realizes Captain Lorca is actually a native of the Mirror Universe. His determination to develop the spore drive is not driven by a desire to win the Federation's war, but by his own ambition to return to the Terran universe and overthrow Emperor Philippa Georgiou.

He also recruits and grooms Burnham to replace the dead Mirror Burnham as his partner in this plot. This proves to be a fatal error. Burnham's loyalty to the Federation instantly destroys any trust she might have had in him, once she realizes who he is. She never loses sight of

her primary mission, to find the intel needed to get *Discovery* safely home and win the war.

Plus, Captain Georgiou was Burnham's mentor for seven years, while she has known Lorca only for a few months. Naturally, she is most drawn to Mirror Georgiou. She also believes that the emperor, who has engineered the defeat of nearly all the Mirror Klingons, can teach the Federation how to defeat its own Klingons.

In accomplishing her own mission, Burnham succeeds in decapitating an Empire which has had stable rule under Georgiou for at least two or three decades. With Lorca dead, Georgiou abducted into the Prime Universe, and much of the Empire's leadership presumably lost in the destruction of the emperor's flagship, the Terran Empire is surely

left with a huge power vacuum.

This first known crossover of personnel between the Mirror and Prime Universes is so consequential that both the Federation and Emperor Georgiou immediately classify all information about the parallel realities. Their motives, however, are very different. Admiral Cornwell reasons that the Federation has suffered devastating loss of life in the war. For too many survivors, the hope that a loved one might still live in a different universe could prove an overwhelming temptation to make the crossover, just to see them again. And the consequences could be catastrophic.

Emperor Georgiou recognizes instantly that the Prime Universe is a deadly ideological threat. She executes on the spot everyone who is present when Burnham discloses

06

her identity. Just the knowledge that such a place as the Federation exists somewhere, with its ideals of democracy, equality, and freedom, would give hope to any subservient race, and add fuel to the rebellion that already threatens the Empire.

The *Enterprise* Incident

This secrecy on both sides helps save the lives of the next Starfleet officers to cross over in 2267. When the *U.S.S. Enterprise* NCC-1701's diplomatic party, led by James T. Kirk, is accidentally transported to the Mirror *Enterprise*, they are, at first, as lost and bewildered as *Discovery*'s crew. Fortunately, the Mirror *Enterprise*'s officers also know nothing about mirror universes, and therefore never suspect that the landing party are impostors. This allows Kirk, McCoy, Scott, and

05 Kirk – posing as Mirror Kirk – with Mirror Spock, in "Mirror, Mirror."

06 Mirror Sulu with Prime Uhura, in "Mirror, Mirror.".

Uhura to maintain their imposture – almost perfectly – until their escape.

Only Mirror Spock and Mirror Marlena identify the intruders, and both ultimately help them to escape, as Spock reasons that each party must be returned to its own universe.

Mirror Spock seems unique among Terran Empire officers. He lacks both the ruthless ambition of the leader, and the fearful subservience of the follower. It's this personality, so familiar to Kirk, that prompts him to make a logical appeal to Mirror Spock, to overturn an empire that is ultimately doomed to fall anyway. Very likely, Mirror Spock's subsequent rise to power is made much easier by the instability that must surely have followed Lorca's failed coup.

Unfortunately for the human race, Kirk's persuasiveness has catastrophic results for the Empire, as described a century later by Intendant Kira of Mirror Terok Nor:

"[Spock] rose to commander in chief of the Empire by preaching reform, disarmament, peace. It was a remarkable turnabout for his people. Unfortunately for them, by the time Spock had completed his reforms, his Empire was in no position to defend itself against us." ("Crossover")

Clearly, Emperor Georgiou's destruction of Firewolf's rebel headquarters was only a temporary setback to rebel movements. They have evolved into the Alliance led by the Klingons and the Cardassians, which finally overthrows the Empire.

An Evil Alliance

In 2370, two Deep Space 9 officers, Major Kira Nerys and Doctor Julian Bashir, are thrown into the Mirror Universe by a wormhole anomaly. There they discover that virtually the entire human race has been enslaved by the Alliance. Since no one on Mirror Terok Nor believes Bashir's claim that he, a member of a slave race, is a doctor, humans have probably had this status for several decades at least.

Mirror Universe Episodes
In chronological order...

Enterprise
"In a Mirror, Darkly, Parts I and II"

Discovery
"Despite Yourself"
"The Wolf Inside"
"Vaulting Ambition"
"What's Past Is Prologue"
(Plus, arguably, the nine other episodes featuring either Mirror Lorca or Mirror Georgiou)

Star Trek
"Mirror, Mirror"

Deep Space Nine
"Crossover"
"Through the Looking Glass"
"Shattered Mirror"
"Resurrection"
"The Emperor's New Cloak"

Hidden History

Gaps in the known history of the Mirror Universe raise some intriguing and unanswered questions...

- Does Mirror Sato succeed in her coup to become emperor? ("In a Mirror, Darkly, Part 2")
- How much does 23rd Century technology from the *Defiant* help the 22nd Century Empire expand its control? Since the Tholians had already stripped the ship, which side wins this futuristic arms race? ("In a Mirror, Darkly")
- Is the rebellion led by "Firewolf," alias Voq, against Emperor Georgiou a direct successor to the rebellion defeated by Mirror Archer 100 years earlier, or is it a new uprising after a period of internal peace? Do the forces of Voq's rebellion later evolve into the Alliance that overthrows the Empire?
- When did Mirror Lorca replace Lorca in the Prime Universe? What has happened to the real Lorca? Did the Mirror *Discovery* also replace *Discovery* in the Prime Universe? If so, what has happened to it?
- Does Mirror Spock start his takeover of the Empire by using the Tantalus Field against Mirror Kirk? Since the Tantalus Field's victims instantly disappear with no sign of disintegration, can it actually be a teleportation device or interdimensional portal? ("Mirror, Mirror")
- How long has the Alliance been in power when Kira and Bashir arrive at Mirror Terok Nor? Is the Alliance enslaving any other races besides Humans? The Ferengi, perhaps, given the fate of the Quark family?
- Does the Alliance survive the capture of the Regent? ("The Emperor's New Cloak")

07

The Intendant tells Kira that she cannot help her return home, nor even allow her to try. There's a protocol, she explains: "After the first crossover, we were afraid others would come and interfere in our affairs. It was decided then that we would immediately dispose of anyone who appeared."

Given the Intendant's fascination with her Mirror twin, she probably would not have let Kira go anyway. Luckily, both Kira and Bashir prove as persuasive as Kirk in convincing discontented Mirror Universe inhabitants that they can resist oppressive regimes. The Mirror Sisko and "Smiley," the Mirror O'Brien, not only help them escape, but flee Terok Nor with Sisko's privateer crew to start a rebellion against the Alliance. ("Crossover")

Prime Sisko has his own opportunity to change Mirror history, when Mirror O'Brien entraps him into crossing over twice, to impersonate Mirror Sisko, who has been killed. On the first crossover, he persuades Mirror Jennifer Sisko to stop developing technology that will help the Alliance destroy the Rebellion. Jennifer changes sides, even though she reveals at the last that his impersonation never actually fooled her. ("Through the Looking Glass")

On his second crossover, Sisko helps another Starfleet ship named *Defiant* tip the balance of power in the Mirror Universe. The Rebellion has built a *Defiant*-class ship from plans Mirror O'Brien stole from Deep Space

07 Mirror Jadzia Dax with "Smiley" O'Brien, in "Through the Looking Glass."

9. Mirror Jennifer lures Jake to cross over, knowing that Sisko will follow his son. Once there, reluctantly, he helps O'Brien finish the *Defiant*, then flies her into battle to defeat a Klingon and Cardassian fleet. This leaves the Rebellion in control of Terok Nor. Tragically for the Sisko men, the victory also leaves Mirror Jennifer dead, as the Intendant kills her while escaping. ("Shattered Mirror")

The last known incursion into the Mirror Universe is initiated by Grand Nagus Zek, who, typically, is looking for new business opportunities. Naturally, the Alliance has no interest in commerce with our universe. Regent Worf takes Zek hostage and demands as ransom Federation cloaking technology, which has never been developed by the Empire or the Alliance.

Yet even the Alliance should know that no one gets the better of a Ferengi in a deal. Quark and Rom go to Zek's rescue, and through a convoluted series of betrayals, they not only free the Nagus, but get the cloaking technology to the Rebellion instead of the Alliance. With it, the Rebellion is able to defeat and capture the Regent himself. ("The Emperor's New Cloak")

This is the latest known event in the Mirror Universe. But we can look ahead and guess that, thanks to one more unintended intervention from the Prime Universe, the balance of power in the Mirror Universe is about to tip. Again. ↓

STAR TREK
DISCOVERY

WISE WORDS

Perhaps more than any other character, Sylvia Tilly is our window on *Star Trek: Discovery's* 23rd-Century universe; her wide-eyed optimism, excitability, undisguised ambition – and tendency to blurt out whatever comes into her head – instantly relatable to 21st-Century viewers. It's an enthusiasm that's shared by the actor who portrays Tilly, Mary Wiseman, herself a relative newbie to television; brimming with excitement about *Trek*, fandom, and her character's journey from cadet, to ensign, to, potentially, command…

Words: Ian Spelling

02

Mary Wiseman can barely contain her enthusiasm – and who could blame her? Here she is, at *Destination Star Trek Germany*, in Dortmund, just moments removed from stepping off the stage after her first *Trek* convention panel. All smiles, her blue eyes wide open, her bright red hair cascading, Wiseman – who plays Sylvia Tilly on *Star Trek: Discovery* – sits down with *Star Trek Magazine* to share her excitement about not just the event, but her entire *Trek* experience so far.

By way of context, Wiseman is at her autograph table, seated next to her *Discovery* co-star and pal, Shazad Latif (Ash Tyler/Voq). They've been playing a game of Patty Cake, this round of which ends with Wiseman winning and declaring, "I went to Juilliard for that!" A look up and down the line finds her in the midst of some remarkable company: William Shatner, Nana Visitor, Robert Duncan McNeill, Nichelle Nichols, Ethan Phillips, Rene Auberjonois, Terry Farrell, Alexander Siddig, Chase Masterson, Aron Eisenberg, *Discovery's* Mary Chieffo (L'Rell) and Kenneth Mitchell (Kol), and many more *Trek* favorites.

03

04

"I'd done the Comic-Con panel last year in San Diego, before the show debuted," Wiseman says, stepping behind a wall to converse in private. "But this, this is completely different. It's more awesome. It's better. It's more fun.

"I didn't get to really interact with the fans at Comic-Con, but this is a weekend with the fans. It's just really nice, really interesting to connect with the people who care so much about this world. Especially, the kids. I've gotten to

01 Mary Wiseman as Sylvia Tilly.

02 Wiseman and Latif play Patty Cake.

03 Tilly and Saru examine Stamets.

04 Killy cosplayer and friends at *Destination Germany.*

05 Hair stylin'.

meet a lot of kids. One of them gave me a gift, a little present, and I had to give her a hug.

"I've seen so many people in 'DISCO' shirts. I'm shocked by how many 'DISCO' shirts I've seen. It's amazing. I love it. *Discovery* has really caught on. It's been so wonderful and I just love the fans so much. It's nice that they are so passionate and so kind, especially the kids, at such a young age.

"And look at all these people," Wiseman enthuses, waving her arms at

the *Trek* celebrities to her left and right. "This is how many years of history?"

Fifty-two.

"Exactly!" the actress exclaims. "It's awesome. It's amazing. What's most amazing is to see so many of the *Deep Space Nine* people here, because it's their 25th anniversary. They've been doing conventions for 25 years, and they're still friends and they know that their show has this sort of legacy. People still love the show and want to meet them. That's hopefully what we're looking down the pike at. I love my cast mates so much. It's actually thrilling to know that we'll be doing this for a really long time into the future."

Wiseman has carved out time to chat with many of her fellow convention guests over the weekend, at their autograph tables, in the green room during breaks, and/or during shuttle rides to and from the hotel where all the *Destination Star Trek Germany* talents are staying. One night at the bar back at the hotel, Wiseman recounts, Nana Visitor sweetly visited the *Discovery* cast – Wiseman, Chieffo, Latif, and Mitchell – and welcomed them to the *Trek* family.

"Nana was talking about exactly what I said, that this is the 25th

anniversary of *Deep Space Nine*, and how we're going to be a part of this family for a very long time," Wiseman says. "So, those loops and those relationships are really important. I've never been a part of anything like this. It's 52 years for some of them. It's not something I was accustomed to up until this point, so this whole experience has been life-changing and incredible for me."

New School

Just as Tilly is a newbie to pretty much everything in outer space and aboard a starship, but is fast adapting to it and its intricacies, Wiseman is a relative acting newcomer who – when it comes to *Star Trek* and its global reach – has been thrown into the deep end of the pool and learned to swim on the fly. She'd performed on stage while in high school and during her time at Boston University – and, later, at Juilliard, where she acted with and befriended future *Discovery* co-star Chieffo. Her early television credits include *Difficult People*, *Longmire*, and *Baskets*, and she

> "I just love the *Star Trek* fans so much. It's nice that they are so passionate and so kind, especially the kids, at such a young age."

made her Broadway stage debut in a 2015 production of *Thérèse Raquin*.

Viewers immediately gravitated toward Tilly, as, arguably more than any other character on the show, she's one of us. She arrived on board the *U.S.S. Discovery* as a young, eager, nervous, excited and excitable character; open-minded, funny as hell, willing to learn, and outspoken, not to mention fully capable of carrying out her duties and ambitious enough to announce her intention of one day settling into the captain's chair aboard a ship.

Over the course of *Discovery*'s first season, Wiseman hit all the right notes in playing Tilly, who learned from and supported Michael Burnham (Sonequa Martin-Green), initially an outsider and distrusted figure, and proved her worthiness to the tough, no-nonsense

LETTING HER HAIR DOWN

Mary Wiseman's hair is a force of nature, and *Discovery*'s powers-that-be, along with the show's hair and make-up team, use it to their advantage, creating different hairstyles for Tilly, and Killy, that fit a particular scene: hair up or hair down, curly or straight, pulled back or loose. *After Trek*, the Matt Mira-hosted post-show analysis, even devoted part of an interstitial segment to the wonders of Wiseman's fiery follicles, noting that she sported nine unique looks in Season 1.

On stage at *Destination Star Trek Germany*, Wiseman jokes that "my hair is the real hero," but talking about it later with *Star Trek Magazine*, she explains, "My hair is not an actor. I think it was just that Tilly came in doing everything by the book. We wanted to have a rigid hairstyle. So, it's very small and pulled back tight. And as we went on, she loosened up. She was bringing more of her personality into it. She's a young person right out of college, basically, so she's experimenting with her look. We all wear the same outfits every day. You'd change your hairstyle, too, just to mix it up."

Stamets (Anthony Rapp), Lorca (Jason Isaacs), and Saru (Doug Jones).

She also won over fans with her alternately humorous and hardened turn as Captain Killy, the Mirror Universe iteration of Tilly. Further, the actress uttered many of the show's best lines, from "I love feeling feelings" to "I used to exclusively go for soldiers, but I'm going through a musician phase right now," and from "What the heck… heck… hell? What the hell! Hold your horses!" to "Insult her again, and your nose is going to be able to sniff the back of your head."

"I loved Season 1," Wiseman explains. "I felt it was excellent. I think the emotional grounding that Sonequa brings to the leading role is so, so important. She is the anchor to the

MARY WISEMAN
FILMOGRAPHY
Senior Server, *Craft & Burn*
  (2 episodes, 2012)
Stacey, *Three Dates*
  (short film, 2014)
Shannon, *Netflix Presents: The
  Characters*, "John Early"
  (1 episode, 2016)
Uncredited character, *Difficult
  People* (1 episode, 2016)
Meg Joyce, *Longmire*
  (7 episodes, 2016–17)
Trinity, *Baskets*
  (3 episodes, 2017–18)
Sylvia Tilly, *Star Trek: Discovery*
  (13 episodes, 2017–18)

06 Tilly with Culber in "Despite Yourself."

07 Wiseman wows the fans at *Destination Germany*.

08 Tilly and Stamets in "Si Vis Pacem, Para Bellum."

whole story, and it's just phenomenal, so rooted in a real, grounded experience coming from her.

"Then, there are lighter bits, that the rest of us kind of fill in, that are fun and give it different colors and flavors. And for me, with Tilly, it was wonderful to start at point A and go to points B, C, D, E, and F, because it gives you somewhere to go. You start out one way. You're not fully formed, not fully ripened, and the audience gets to see you learn and grow. That's a really gratifying experience for me and I hope it is for the audience as well."

From Tilly to Killy

So, what Tilly beats did Wiseman most enjoy bringing to life? "She started fresh out of the Academy," Wiseman replies. "She doesn't have a lot of friends. She meets Michael Burnham, who is incredibly different from her, but also a genius and very experienced. I think she learned a lot from Michael, and they

> "A lot of crazy things happened, and those crises really forced Tilly to grow up fast and access parts of her personality that she didn't even know she had."

got into a lot of trouble. A lot of crazy things happened, and those crises really forced Tilly to grow up fast and access parts of her personality that she didn't even know she had.

"Becoming Killy was probably the most fun," the actor continues. "I wouldn't say it was challenging – it was just really fun. Everybody else around me is a huge badass, and it was Tilly's one moment to be a badass, too. And doing that with Jonathan Frakes [who directed 'Despite Yourself'] was awesome and a great experience.

"The episode that was really challenging would be ['The Wolf Inside'], the one where she's trying to bring Stamets back to life. There was a lot of jargon, but it was also an operatic, emotional journey for Tilly. It was her finding her power and telling Saru, 'This is what needs to happen,' and then finding a way to bring Stamets back. So, that was challenging, but it was really cool."

And, while it was a kick to play Killy, having done so may carry over to Tilly's evolution. Tilly was merely posing as Killy, but now she comprehends what she's capable of. "I think she accessed parts of her that she hadn't been forced to access before," Wiseman observes, expounding on a point she made moments ago. "It asked different things of her, and I think from that moment onwards you saw a stronger Tilly. She stood up to people, she was more confident about her skills and talents, and she still had a huge heart and led with kindness, but I think she now also knows how to get her voice out there.

"What's funny to me is some people think of Tilly and Killy as two separate people. Actually, we haven't seen Killy. We've only seen Tilly pretending to be Killy. She did what she thinks Killy is, based on some data."

Drop the F-bomb

Contemplating Season 1 highlights, Wiseman speaks generally and specifically. She adores the entire *Discovery* cast, calling them "incredibly kind and fun and funny people," and adding: "It's a pleasure to go to work

> ## "I trust our writers, and the things they've told me are going to happen are really exciting."

every day and see them." She also treasured the entertaining, Easter Egg-y moment she shared with Clint Howard in "Will You Take My Hand?" In that episode, the freshman year finale, Tilly got drugged and robbed by an Orion played by Howard, a frequent *Trek* guest star who made his first appearance as a child actor decades ago, when he portrayed Balok in the original series installment "The Corbomite Maneuver." Laughing, Wiseman says, "Oh, it was so wild doing that scene with Clint. I got to get high with Clint Howard. It was surreal and really silly and fun. It was such a pleasure to work with him."

And let's not forget that, in Season 1, Wiseman delivered a *Trek* first. She, as Tilly, dropped *Star Trek*'s first ever F-bomb. She did so in "Choose Your Pain," during the scene in which Tilly, Burnham, and Stamets recognized the

connection between the tardigrade/ Ripper and the mycelial network. "No one was like, 'You dropped the first F-bomb,'" the actress notes. "I wasn't thinking about it that way. We weren't talking about it that way on set. It just felt organic to the character, organic to the moment.

"Actually, it was one of the first moments where Tilly and Stamets connected, and he took on more of a mentor role with her. Stamets can be allergic to levity and the joyful quirkiness that Tilly brings, but that was the moment where he really saw her and was able to appreciate that. And their relationship has grown. Now, they're able to appreciate the differences between them."

With *Discovery* Season 2 heading for an early 2019 debut, Tilly is also the focus of one of the four *Star Trek: Short Treks* that will air in the run-up to the second season. Much like the show's fans, Wiseman is eager to discover what's in store for both Tilly and *Discovery*.

"I trust our writers, and the things they've told me are going to happen are really exciting," Wiseman concludes. "I think people are going to love it." ✦

STAR TREK
DISCOVERY

HALL OF MIRRORS

When the *U.S.S. Discovery* breached the dimensional barrier and plunged into the Mirror Universe, among the simmering subplots that were brought to the boil was the mystery surrounding Lieutenant Ash Tyler. For actor Shazad Latif, that trip to another dimension marked the culmination of months of work playing not just Tyler, but the Klingon Voq – and introduced yet another character into the mix, in the shape of Mirror Voq…

Words: Mark Newbold

Star Trek Magazine: What are your thoughts and emotions on that Mirror Universe sequence of episodes at the back end of *Discovery* Season 1?
Shazad Latif: ["The Wolf Inside"] was a crazy episode to film, because we spent two separate days filming the big scene with Mirror Voq, which was so much fun. It came out of the blue; we were never sure if we were going to be able to get to do that. It was great to have [Voq] speak English, and meet this version of Voq, this rebel leader. And then to fight yourself, fight Tyler – it was madness; this inner battle played out in physical form.

There were so many things going on in that episode, it was full on. Then the whole thing with Sonequa, and pretending to be Terrans… It was full of internal struggle and external struggle.

When you saw it on the page and realized you were literally fighting yourself – which is a classic *Trek* theme – how did you address the practicalities of doing that? Presumably in reality there was another guy in the fight?
Yeah, there was. That's crazy in itself. The other guy had learned the fight, so the first day, we did Voq, so that all the main

close-ups and the main shots were Voq. Obviously some of the wide shots had to be the stunt double, but I did all of the fighting. In that scene Tyler doesn't really say that much, so the other guy played Tyler so that he could learn my movements for Voq, and then the next day when we did it the other way round, he could just do that and I could give him pointers and say, "I did this with my arm," or whatever, so he did a lot of work himself.

So there was Tyler guy, the guy dressed up the next day as Mirror Voq, and then stunt Voq for the fight. It was pretty crazy.

Was it like learning a dance?
Yeah, especially the fight stuff, because it was a small space and there were lots of people around, so we were hitting cups and saucers everywhere in a very small space. You could easily hit someone with one of the bat'leths, so you've got to be on it. It was sweaty in there; it was one of the hottest days that we filmed on.

Where did you film the scene?
It was actually in the back lot [in Toronto, where *Discovery* is filmed], but they made it look like this sort of little desert realm. It was insane, a crazy day.

Both characters, Tyler and Voq, had huge character arcs. As an actor, you'd have probably been happy with either character, but to get both must have felt like you'd won the lottery.
Yeah, because I knew I'd be getting to explore not just one side, not just the action hero arc or the dark

"The Wolf Inside"
Star Trek: Discovery, Season 1, Episode 11
Written by: Lisa Randolph
Directed by: TJ Scott
First aired: January 14, 2018
Undercover as her Mirror Universe counterpart aboard the *I.S.S. Shenzhou*, Michael Burnham opts to meet with the leader of a group of rebels fighting the Terran Empire, in order to learn how he united Klingons with other races. That commander turns out to be the Mirror version of Voq, whose words provoke Tyler into a failed assault on the Klingon commander. Later, Burnham confronts Tyler and learns that her lover is, in fact, the Voq of her universe, surgically altered and imprinted with Tyler's memories…

01 Tyler tangles with Mirror Voq, in "The Wolf Inside."

02 Tyler with Burnham, in "Despite Yourself."

03 Shazad Latif on stage at *Destination Star Trek Germany* 2018.

"To fight yourself, fight Tyler – it was madness; this inner battle played out in physical form."

alien character arc. When you put the two together you get this huge amalgamation of something beautifully crazy. To play both is an actor's dream; I don't think I'll ever get to explore something in 15 acts like that in as much depth. It was a goldmine.

With a little distance from Season 1, where does your heart now sit? Do you feel for Voq, or do you feel for Tyler?
Well, the thing is, because I started off as Voq, that was the beginning of the thread, and that's the underlying thing. I can't choose between them, because each of them has an equally justifiable case. Neither is good or bad. It's a tough one.

And when you walk away at the end of "Will You Take My Hand?", is that Tyler walking away, or is it Voq?
I feel like it's both. It's Tyler realizing that he has to accept Voq as part of him, so it's him being the bigger

person. I've got to leave Michael Burnham behind because I'm only causing her harm, so I think that Tyler's making that big of a decision there.

When you encounter Mirror Voq, he's been on rather a different journey…
Yeah, he's this rebel leader on this great world where everyone comes together. I'd like to see him again, because there's a sense that he got off that planet. That's an interesting thing that we could explore.

Mirror Voq brings to mind Chancellor Gorkon from *Star Trek VI: The Undiscovered Country*. Gorkon is an ambassador for peace; could Mirror Voq be the same?
If Tyler is going back to the Klingons with L'Rell, then they're going to have to sort some stuff out and play that ambassador role, in a sense. If Tyler meets Mirror Voq again, they could figure out some kind of peace. I don't know what's going to happen.

Would you like to touch on the Mirror concept again in the future?
Yeah, I really like that character. He was a lot of fun to play, because there was a power about him, there was a dignity about the character. I like playing him.

VOQ STAR!

Words: Ian Spelling

"I can't believe I get to be a part of this," exclaims Shazad Latif, speaking to *Star Trek Magazine* at *Destination Star Trek Germany*, in Dortmund. "It's so unreal to me." Waving his hands in front of him as he speaks these words, from his vantage point he can see nearly 30 fellow *Star Trek* celebrities, two busy activities stages, numerous vendor booths, and thousands of *Star Trek* fans, many sporting *Discovery* uniforms or DISCO T-shirts.

What was the biggest surprise, not in terms of shooting, but in terms of fandom, meeting people and expectations?
It was that I didn't realize how big the fandom really is. I knew a little. I'd gotten a taste of it. But when you start coming to conventions, you really see it. This is my second one, and I know the Germans really love *Star Trek* and are really loving *Discovery*. So, all the world is discovering the show. I never pictured myself taking photos or signing autographs. I didn't ever know that that would happen for me in my career. So, it's very beautiful; it's lovely to meet people who are passionate about the show.

How ready are you to have *Star Trek* be a part of your life from here on in? You're seeing some of the people here at *Destination Star Trek Germany*. There are members of the original cast, and they're into their 52nd year of this. *Deep Space Nine* is celebrating its 25th anniversary…
I think it's exciting as hell. It's great. If me and the two Marys and Kenneth and Sonequa and Doug and Jason are all here in 50 years, I think that would be a beautiful, beautiful thing. We're very close anyway, all of us, just by the nature of the show. We were there for 10 months, the first season. So, I think that's a very nice thing, a bonus, for all of us.

You've got a Voq pin right now on your shirt. How cool is that, to wear… yourself?
I just got this today. This is the first time I've seen it. I want to give one to my nieces and nephews, but I'm actually enjoying it. I looked at it and I went, "Er, I'll get them another one, because I really want this one." I like the fact he's got a bit of a beard, because when I'm shaved I look like a strange alien. I look like Voq.

He didn't feel as much of an outsider as Prime Voq.
He was a very strong leader, and it was nice to play that because Voq was very quiet and humble – not powerful.

How has your experience been on this show? Has it been way above your expectations?
A year and a half ago I was doing an audition tape and I didn't know that technically I'd be playing four characters in 10 months. It's been a rollercoaster really. It's been brilliant, to play this.

Do you like losing yourself in characters?
That's the joy of it. That's what we do – we're playing, in a sense. Children take play very seriously. It's all about finding that balance.

You've had a bit of downtime between seasons; what have you been up to?
I do a lot of writing with friends of mine, partly for bonding and also to see if we can create things together. Hopefully that's a good journey to go on. I've been cold water swimming – I've been reading a lot of Wim Hof. I've been going to the local lido and ponds. I used to be a night owl and now I'm trying to be an early bird. I've been trying to get into good habits – have a little health kick, lose the little belly that shows up in the uniforms! ⋆

MUDD'S RAINN

An undoubted highlight of the first season of *Star Trek: Discovery* was Rainn Wilson's turn as incorrigible galactic rogue Harry Mudd. Building on Roger C. Carmel's iconic original series portrayal, Wilson also got the chance to direct himself as Mudd in a *Short Trek* – and given half a chance, he'd happily continue his reign as Harry.

WORDS: IAN SPELLING

"I'm about the biggest sci-fi fan that you could imagine, because my dad was a science fiction writer," explains Rainn Wilson, referring to author Robert Wilson, who wrote 1978 pulp SF novel *Tentacles of Dawn*. "So, I grew up with it. We read science fiction all the time. I saw *2001: A Space Odyssey* when I was maybe four years old, and that blew my mind."

And, yes, confirms the versatile actor – who has a recurring role on *Star Trek: Discovery* as Harcourt Fenton Mudd – *Star Trek* entered his orbit at an early age. He'd arrive home from school, plop down on the couch, and watch Kirk, Spock, McCoy, and the rest of the *U.S.S. Enterprise* crew in action via reruns of the original series. Even better, his local television station aired *Star Trek* reruns repeatedly on weekends.

02

03

"I'm talking maybe as early as '71, '72, '73, definitely," Wilson recalls. "So, the original series had just gone off the air. It's an odd thing, because… I was just thinking about this: now, because of the internet, and because of conventions, you can find your tribe. I remember there was a time I was really into the band R.E.M. I loved R.E.M. – I had all their albums, I memorized their lyrics, and I just thought they were amazing. I was in a record shop once, and I found an R.E.M. fanzine. I picked it up, and it said something like 'This is for R.E.M. fans.' It was hand-printed, mimeographed, or something like that, by some fans in Georgia. I paid $3.50 for it. It was incredible, because it [made me realize], 'Oh, there's other people that feel the way that I do. There's people dissecting the lyrics, and people talking about what their favorite albums are, and drawing

01 Rainn Wilson as Harry Mudd in his debut *Discovery* appearance, Season 1, Episode 5, "Choose Your Pain.

02 Mudd in captivity again in the *Short Trek* "The Escape Artist."

03 Mudd captures Stamets and Burnham in Episode 7, "Magic to Make the Sanest Man Go Mad."

artwork inspired by R.E.M.' It was so touching to me."

Again, that was all pre-internet – practically the Stone Age. Message boards didn't exist. Neither did chat rooms. No one could text or instant message like-minded friends about exciting news or compelling rumors.

"You couldn't find that community," Wilson puts it succinctly. "So now, there's this [*Star Trek*] community, but even back then I went to Norwescon – which is a science-fiction convention – several times. My dad had written *Tentacles of Dawn*, and I would go play *Dungeons*

& Dragons there, and I would go to the panels. They had a 24-hour movie room, movie marathons playing constant sci-fi movies, and horror and stuff like that. I still have my science fiction book collection from the '70s, which numbers about 3,400 science fiction books. So, I was – I am – a huge, huge fan."

To the Disco

Cut to the present. Wilson, now in his early 50s, is a three time Emmy Award-nominated actor. He's best known for his role as Dwight Schrute on the American iteration of *The*

> ## "Harry Mudd is a conman, smuggler, raconteur, roustabout, and it is really informed by his wardrobe."
>
> RAINN WILSON

05

Office, but he's frequently lent his talents to sci-fi and horror films and shows, as well as several animated projects – and by frequently, we really mean frequently: *Galaxy Quest*, *Charmed*, *Dark Angel*, *House of 1,000 Corpses*, *My Super Ex-Girlfriend*, *The Last Mimzy*, *Monsters vs. Aliens*, *Transformers: Revenge of the Fallen*, *Super*, *Cooties*, *Uncanny*, *Smurfs: The Lost Village*, *Mowgli*, *The Death of*

Superman, and the newly released animated feature *Batman: Hush*, with Wilson as the voice of Lex Luthor.

Wilson very much wanted to add *Star Trek* to his résumé, particularly since acting with Patrick Stewart in a 1995 Broadway production of *The Tempest* doesn't quite count. Right after CBS All Access announced that *Discovery* was in the works, the actor reached out to his agent expressing his

04 Strung up in "The Escape Artist."

05 With cellmate Tyler in "Choose Your Pain."

desire to beam aboard. Wilson met the *Discovery* team, which had nothing for him, at least initially. Six months later, though, he received the offer to play Harry Mudd, the fast-talking, chaos-causing criminal and conman.

Mudd in Your I

Wilson went on to portray Mudd in the first-season episodes "Choose Your Pain" and "Magic to Make the Sanest Man Go Mad." In the former, Mudd spent much of his time in a prison cell, clashing with Gabriel Lorca (Jason Isaacs) and Ash Tyler (Shazad Latif), grousing about the Klingon-Federation war, and pining for his beloved Stella. In the latter, a time-looping Mudd assumed command of the *U.S.S. Discovery*, killed Lorca several times, and delivered a barrage of savage one-liners. Between Seasons 1 and 2 of *Discovery*, Wilson returned to play Mudd again in the *Star Trek: Short Treks* installment "The Escape Artist," which he also directed.

"I think finding that edge to Mudd," Wilson replies when asked what worked best for him about his

06

07

first two episodes. "How dastardly can you be, and at the same time, how much humor and comedy and charm can he bring? Finding that balance is always interesting with Mudd. I think that they walked that tightrope really well. He was a little more comedic at first, and then we saw in 'Magic to Make the Sanest Man Go Mad' how he turned and there was a real edge to this Harry Mudd. He was not quite so much a buffoon, but he has to be believable as a real threat."

06 Reunited with his betrothed, Stella, in "Magic to Make the Sanest Man Go Mad."

07 With Lorca in "Choose Your Pain."

Colorful Clothes

It's been said that clothes make the man. Well, they also make the Mudd. Just as Roger C. Carmel's colorful attire in the original series complemented the actor's broad, playful performance as Mudd, so too have Wilson's elaborate threads on *Discovery*. At the mention of *Discovery* costume designer Gersha Phillips' name, Wilson immediately heaps words of praise upon her.

"She's brilliant," he enthuses. "She's phenomenal. These costumes are next-level *Star Trek* stuff, and I'm not just saying that. I really think they're exquisite and her designs are immaculate.

"Costumes always help you find your character. Dwight Schrute has a polyester suit, has got a calculator wristwatch. He wears a beeper, even though beepers are defunct, because he didn't want to give up his beeper. He's wearing one as late as 2013, when the show ended. Harry Mudd is almost part pirate. It's a little operatic: leather boots, a lot of buckles and straps and rings. It feels very ornate. He's kind of conman, smuggler, raconteur, roustabout, and it is really informed by his wardrobe."

A Shorter Trek

Discussions with *Discovery*'s producers about Wilson possibly returning to the show in Season 2 led to him directing "The Escape Artist." He read the script for the short, which he deemed "absolutely hysterical and strange and exciting," and then was invited to direct it.

"It was an incredible learning opportunity," he says. "I'd directed three episodes of *The Office* before, but *The Office* was pretty simple. It's like, 'Where are you going to put the camera, to cover the dialogue and the desks?' We used documentary-style cameras on *The Office*. This one was a lot more demanding.

"I got to learn a ton about visual effects and special effects, and how

08

09

08 Another sticky situation for Harry, in "The Escape Artist."

09 Wilson stepped behind the camera for "The Escape Artist," directing the *Short Trek*.

> "Mudd was a little more comedic at first, and then we saw in 'Magic to Make the Sanest Man Go Mad' how he turned and there was a real edge to this Harry Mudd."
>
> RAINN WILSON

visual effects work, what it is when you do a plate shot and you have multiple Mudds in that plate shot. There were just so many visual post aspects that I needed to become acquainted with, and they have such a huge, amazing team there.

"We were shooting 'The Escape Artist' when they were shooting the last episode of *Discovery*'s second season," Wilson reveals. "So, we were there right at the end of it. I got to use their wardrobe department and their hair and make-up department,

Mudd: In His Shoes

Rainn Wilson has been here before: inheriting a role originated unforgettably by a predecessor. First, for the American version of *The Office*, he assumed the part of Dwight Schrute from Mackenzie Crook; and long before Wilson played Harry Mudd on *Discovery*, the esteemed Roger C. Carmel appeared as the character in the original series episodes "Mudd's Women" and "I, Mudd" (and provided the voice of Mudd in the *Star Trek: The Animated Series* episode "Mudd's Passion").

"Basically, I stole all of the brilliant stuff that [Crook] did, and then added my own stuff, and it was great," Wilson says of *The Office*. "And it's the same thing with [*Discovery*]. I inherited a character that had been previously played by another brilliant actor. I stole a lot of things that I loved from his performance, and then added a lot more of my own.

"It's a testament to [Carmel]; what an interesting actor he was. You can't take your eyes off him when he's in an episode – so full of light. There is a wonderful light and dark quality that the original writers brought to [Mudd]. But I think the new writers [on *Discovery*] have also brought their [own spin]. He's mischievous and deadly at the same time, and that's a fun balance to watch."

10

and their special effects and visual effects and set design, plus their composers and everything like that. It feels like a multi-multi-million-dollar production.

"I think it was also a challenge to find that balance of, 'This has to be really funny and entertaining, and it also has to feel really real,'" Wilson continues. "The stakes have to be high. It's not just a comedy in the same way that *Guardians of the Galaxy* has some outrageous visual fun and great jokes and one-liners; you have to care about the characters and you have to believe that you're in the real world with Harry, even as outlandish as it is."

Multiple Mudds

There were plenty more challenges on "The Escape Artist": envisioning visual effects to be added later, particularly during the sequences with multiple Mudds; hanging suspended in the air for take after take; and, perhaps trickiest of all, acting and directing at the same time.

"You have to call 'Cut,' and then you have to run over to a little

10 Roger C. Carmel as Harry Mudd in "Mudd's Women."

monitor and watch the last take and watch your performance, and make sure it's fitting in with everyone else's performances," Wilson notes. "But you're also keeping an eye on everything else, like where the camera is, how tight the frame is, and you're thinking, 'Is everything happening in the right order? Are we telling the story that we need to tell?'

"It's incredibly challenging being on both sides of the camera, but boy, it sure is fun. Fortunately, I'd played Mudd a couple of times, so I really knew the character pretty well, and I knew how I wanted to play him."

Fan reaction to "The Escape Artist" proved to be quite positive. It was a fast-paced, entertaining romp with a couple of neat twists. Wilson sounds as if he liked it, too. "I'm really thrilled," he says. "To be honest, I think it's f***ing awesome. I think it's exciting and visually cool. I got so much support from the producers, and so much help from an amazing crew up there. The cast was fantastic. I couldn't be happier with how it turned out."

Another Trek?

Wilson is currently hard at work on his next project, an American adaptation of the British series, *Utopia*, in which he'll co-star with John Cusack and Sasha Lane. Also on the way are the films *Robodog*, *Blackbird*, and *Don't Tell a Soul*. Considering that most of the *U.S.S. Discovery* crew warped deep into the future in the *Star Trek: Discovery* second-season finale, it's anyone's guess as to whether or not Mudd will – or even could – wreak more havoc in Season 3. Wilson, for his part, hopes for a revisit, and even has a few ideas about the next steps in Mudd's development as a character.

"I would love to be back on the show," he says. "I would love to do more *Star Trek* and more Harry Mudd. I think the evolution is keeping the audience on their toes. You don't know if you're supposed to be laughing or if you're supposed to be afraid for your life. He's a master of illusion. He's a conman, and nothing is ever as it seems to be with Harry Mudd. That's what's really exciting about him, and I hope that we're able to play with that aspect of his character in the future." ✦

The Ties That Bind

From *Star Trek: Discovery* to
the original series… and beyond

DISCO

U.S.S. ENTERPRISE 1701

>TREK

With the introduction of Spock, Pike, and Number One, the ties between *Star Trek: Discovery* and the original series are only strengthening as Season 2 of the prequel show unfolds. But there are ties to – and differences from – other eras of *Trek*, too, both in-universe and behind the camera, from serialized storytelling to Section 31. *Star Trek Magazine* unpicks the ties that bind.

Words: K. Stoddard Hayes

The second *Star Trek* series to take place before the original series, *Star Trek: Discovery*'s 10-year gap to *Star Trek* presents as many creative and continuity challenges as the century between *Star Trek: Enterprise* and *Star Trek*. At the same time, in the real world, the half century between the production of *Star Trek* and the production of *Discovery* has a major impact of its own. So, with *Discovery* Season 2's increased links to the original series, where does the show fit in *Star Trek* history – real and imaginary? And how does it connect to the nearest series in the timeline, *Star Trek*?

Network or Syndicated

Star Trek began as a network series, in a decade when the networks still broadcast the majority of scripted shows. However, network distribution has not always been kind to *Star Trek*. Thanks to bad scheduling decisions and

low ratings, the original series got its third season on NBC only after intense fan lobbying. By 1995, smaller networks like UPN needed far fewer viewers to make a series a ratings success. Even so, of the network *Treks*, only *Star Trek: Voyager* finished a complete seven-season run; its successor, *Enterprise*, struggled continually with ratings and was canceled after only four seasons.

Syndication proved a much more successful broadcast platform. Nightly syndicated reruns of the original series, beginning soon after its final network broadcast, expanded *Star Trek*'s audience so fast that within a few years, Paramount was ready to risk funding more *Star Trek*, and the movie franchise was born. Less than 10 years after that, the first of the new TV series, *Star Trek: The Next Generation*, also became a hit in first-run syndication. Its success brought *Star Trek* back to the small screen continuously for nearly two decades.

01

02

Streaming: the Future

In the years since the 2004 cancellation of *Enterprise*, television distribution has changed dramatically. Premium cable channels and streaming services draw a growing segment of viewing audiences away from network television, and usually capture the majority of the industry's creative awards as well. Given that the previous *Star Trek* series were already profitable on CBS All Access, *Discovery*'s distribution as a streaming-only series should not be a surprising business decision – though it may have disappointed some fans accustomed to getting *Star Trek* for free in their cable TV line-up.

The decision to move to streaming has also had an artistic impact. After 50 years of studio insistence on episodic storylines, the showrunners were able to bring fully serialized storytelling to *Discovery*. This is, of course, the current standard for 21st Century television drama. However, it's very new for *Star Trek*.

No other *Star Trek* series has been completely serialized. *Enterprise*'s third season is the only previous time an entire *Star Trek* season has been devoted to one storyline. Before that, the nearest

01 Captain Kirk and the crew of the *Enterprise* in the network television series *Star Trek*...

02 ...and Captain Archer and the crew of the *Enterprise* in the network television series *Enterprise*.

03 George Takei as Hikaru Sulu.

04 Anthony Rapp as Paul Stamets.

05 Kirk, Burnham, and Archer: uniform evolution... or rather, devolution.

example was *Star Trek: Deep Space Nine*'s Dominion War arc, spanning multiple seasons, with some storylines taking up four, five, or more episodes.

Streaming distribution also freed *Star Trek* from television broadcast content restrictions for the first time. *Discovery* does not shy away from portraying graphic violence on occasion – not least Tyler's horrific flashbacks – leading to a lot of critical debate over whether this much blood and gore is really right for *Trek*.

There is even – gasp! – swearing, when, in "Choose Your Pain," Tilly and Stamets agree that piloting through the mycelial network is "f***ing cool!" Oddly, this little word seems to bother some fans and critics even more than the violence. Just as odd, considering the amount of blood splashed on the screen, one former showrunner ventured in interviews that nudity doesn't really fit with *Star Trek*. Gruesome violence? Fine. F-bombs? Well, maybe once a season. Nudity? No way!

Where No Cast Has Gone Before

Star Trek pioneered diversity in its casting and characters, and has never

deviated from that commitment. In the 1960s, the casting of a Japanese-American and an African-American to play military professionals rather than racial stereotypes was transformative, especially for viewers of varied ethnicity. In the 21st Century, *Discovery*'s multi-ethnic cast, while completely traditional for *Star Trek*, has become much more of a norm for television casting in general.

Discovery's casting does look a little different from previous series, though. In the earlier series, actors often played human characters of specific nationalities that matched their own heritage. Uhura is a Swahili-speaking African native; O'Brien is Irish; Chakotay is Native American; the Siskos are from New Orleans, a city famous for its rich African-American culture.

Discovery's actors, diverse in their own ethnic backgrounds, don't seem to be portraying any specific ethnicity or culture; they are all fairly generic Starfleet. Even Sonequa Martin-Green's Burnham isn't African-American by culture: she was raised as a Vulcan.

The big diversity breakthrough in *Discovery* comes in its portrayal of Hugh Culber and Paul Stamets as the

03

04

Uniformity

Make-up and costume design are two areas where even *Star Trek* canon must give way to the realities of film and TV production. Even so, the difference between *Discovery*'s Starfleet uniforms in 2256, and those seen on Kirk's *Enterprise* in 2266, led to much fan debate, especially since the *Kelvin* Timeline characters do wear an update of the traditional uniforms. But consider this: the differences between *Discovery*'s sleek navy blue uniforms, with their metallic accents, and the original *Star Trek* velour tunics in their three colors, is no greater than the difference between the velour shirts and the red-and-white wool jackets of *Star Trek II: The Wrath of Khan*.

In the absence of any official in-universe rationale (like *Enterprise*'s explanation for the changing Klingon foreheads), we might put this uniform change down to our hypothetical "leave the war behind" policy. Christopher Pike is the first *Discovery* character to appear in the gold command tunic of the 2260s. Perhaps the Admiralty decided that the blue uniforms had too many associations with the tragic war, and should be phased out. As a bonus, the production of tens of thousands of new uniforms would boost the post-war economy by providing a lot of work in the clothing and textile industries!

After the war, the Klingons will also give up their massive plated armor in favor of leaner-looking uniforms with metallic fabrics and leather. Perhaps the Klingons discovered during the war that their bulky shoulder plates, made for battling other heavily armored Klingons, are too cumbersome for hand-to-hand against sleekly clad Starfleet officers. Within the next couple of decades, the Klingons will also realize that they look much scarier with a lot of hair!

Star Trek pioneered diversity in its casting and characters, and has never deviated from that commitment.

first same-sex couple in a *Star Trek* series. To the dismay of many fans, the relationship seemed to fall to the pernicious trope of on-screen same-sex relationships always ending tragically, when Culber was murdered by Tyler ("Despite Yourself"). However, the actors and the showrunners have all stated that this is not the end of the relationship, nor the last we will see of Culber.

Command Decision

Discovery's character line-up makes an even bigger departure from the long-standing *Star Trek* format. For the first time, the main character is not the captain. Having the protagonist be the first officer changes the range of dramatic choices available to her.

05

Everything We Know About Christopher Pike

Born in Mojave, California in the 2220s, Pike joins Starfleet and serves on the *U.S.S. Enterprise* under Captain April for several years. By 2254, he is in command.

In 2254, the *Enterprise* encounters the Talosians, who take Pike captive in an attempt to use him as breeding stock for their "zoo" ("The Cage").

By 2255, Pike is renowned as one of Starfleet's most decorated captains ("Choose Your Pain"). Presumably he commands the *Enterprise* throughout the Klingon War, bringing her successfully through any engagements.

In 2256, he is given temporary command of the *U.S.S. Discovery* for a mission to seek out and determine the source and intent of seven mysterious signals that have been detected across the galaxy. Most likely he will return to the *Enterprise* afterward.

In the early 2260s, he is promoted to Fleet Captain and leaves the *Enterprise* to James Kirk. During a training mission on an aging ship, he rescues a number of cadets from a radiation disaster, an episode which leaves him completely paralyzed, unable even to speak.

In 2267, Spock commandeers the *Enterprise* to take Pike back to Talos IV at the invitation of the Talosians. There, Pike is able to experience his remaining years free of his injuries, thanks to the Talosian technology of illusion ("The Menagerie, Parts I and II").

Starfleet will later name a prestigious medal in his honor: the Christopher Pike Medal of Valor. This is surely inspired by the act of heroism and sacrifice which crippled him, and probably by other actions as well ("Tears of the Prophets").

09

06

07

08

Starship captains take direct orders only from admirals, who are seldom around. First officers have to take orders from their captains all the time, and see that those orders are carried out by the entire crew as well. And they must do so even when they strongly disagree with those orders.

Burnham's catastrophic failure in this most fundamental of the first officer's duties puts her into another unprecedented role for a *Star Trek* hero. For most of the first season, she is not a first officer, but a convicted mutineer on parole, allowed out of the brig only because Lorca believes she can help him. She has no authority, no input into any decision-making, and she can be stripped of even her freedom at any moment, just on the word of a senior officer.

She also faces the intractable hostility of military personnel for mutineers, deserters, and others who

violate their oaths, though this hostility begins to dissipate rather soon. In the real world, Burnham's conviction might make any friendly crew relationships difficult or impossible, and her contributions to the end of the war would likely earn her no more than a commutation of her sentence, or at best a pardon. Her return to full duty as first officer in "Will You Take My Hand?" seems more of a dramatic convenience – like a disgraced but heroic cadet being given command of a starship at the end of *Star Trek (2009)*.

Ways of the Warriors

When the Klingons first appear in *Discovery*, they are fractured into feuding Houses constantly forming and breaking alliances with each other. Only the messianic leader T'Kuvma, a follower of Kahless, grasps the potential of a united Klingon Empire. Seeing the Federation as the greatest threat

of creating a united Empire. All the Klingons whom Kirk and his crew meet during the Five Year Mission present themselves not as members of individual Houses, but as Klingon officers whose only loyalty is to the Empire ("The Trouble with Tribbles," "Day of the Dove").

At this time, the newly reunited Empire is also embracing imperialist expansion and the possibility of another war with the Federation. And why not, since the last war was such a success? Only the enforced peace of the powerful Organians stops the Empire from another "glorious" war.

> The Klingons whom Kirk and his crew meet during the Five Year Mission present themselves not as members of individual Houses, but as Klingon officers whose only loyalty is to the Empire.

Post-Traumatic Stress

On the Federation side, that first war is far from glorious. Bloodied by tens of thousands of military and civilian casualties, and the loss of entire colonies, the Federation would have lost the war altogether but for the last minute actions of Burnham and Emperor Georgiou ("Will You Take My Hand?"). Yet 10 years later, the Federation, too, seems to have made a complete recovery.

After a devastating war – especially a losing war – a nation usually needs years, even decades, to recover from physical and emotional damage. So it's hard to reconcile this recent war with the powerful Starfleet and prosperous Federation we see during *Star Trek*. Virtually every officer above the rank of ensign would have served in that war, lost many comrades, and survived terrible battles. Some would have lost homes and families as well.

For real-world production reasons there is, of course, no mention in

to Klingon identity, he provokes war as a way to unite the Houses against a common enemy ("The Vulcan Hello," "Battle at the Binary Stars"). After his death in the war's very first battle, Klingon unity soon fractures again as the Houses begin competing with each other to attack Federation assets.

While the feuding Houses devastate the Federation, T'Kuvma's vision seems forgotten by all but a few of his followers, notably L'Rell and Voq. By giving L'Rell the control of Emperor Georgiou's hydro bomb, which can destroy Qo'noS, Burnham provides the leverage L'Rell needs to end the war, and assert control over all the Houses ("Will You Take My Hand?").

Eleven years later, when the *U.S.S. Enterprise* encounters the Klingons at Organia ("Errand of Mercy"), it appears that L'Rell – likely helped by Tyler/Voq and her own passionate commitment – has accomplished T'Kuvma's dream

06 *Discovery*'s Klingons...

07 ...versus the original series' original version.

08 The *Kelvin* Timeline movies played a key role in reinvigorating *Star Trek*.

09 Jeffrey Hunter as Captain Pike.

10 James Frain as *Discovery*'s Sarek.

10

Everything We Know About Sarek's Family Before 2255

Sarek, son of Skon, is the distinguished scion of a distinguished Vulcan family of diplomats and scientists. Born in 2165 on Vulcan, he will serve as a diplomat for most of his life. Around 2227, he spends some years as Vulcan Ambassador to Earth, where he meets and marries the human woman Amanda Grayson.

He has two sons: Sybok, the child of his first marriage to a Vulcan princess, and Spock, son of his second marriage, to Amanda. Both his sons are a disappointment to him. Sybok rebels against Vulcan philosophy by seeking meaning in his emotions as well as in logic (*Star Trek V: The Final Frontier*). Spock endures bullying and prejudice against his half-human nature throughout childhood. To escape it, he rejects a higher education on Vulcan, and enrolls in Starfleet Academy.

Around 2230, Sarek and Amanda adopt the human orphan Michael Burnham, and give her a traditional Vulcan education. When Burnham's school is bombed by terrorists, Sarek revives her from clinical death by a mind meld that transfers a piece of his katra to her. This will later allow the two to communicate telepathically over interstellar distances.

Burnham's academic distinction qualifies her for the Vulcan Expeditionary Group. However, its leaders do not want to accept a human, so they force Sarek to choose between Burnham and Spock. He nominates Spock and tells Burnham she did not qualify. Spock's later decision to join Starfleet instead causes Sarek even greater pain.

Soon after Burnham's rejection, Sarek brings her to Captain Georgiou, who will be her mentor as she enters Starfleet.

Everything We Know About Section 31 Before 2257

Section 31, the black ops division of Starfleet Intelligence, was created under Starfleet Charter Article 14, Section 31, before the founding of the Federation. Its existence is one of the best-kept secrets in the Federation.

In 2154, Section 31 operative Harris recruits Malcolm Reed to interfere with a Starfleet investigation into the Klingon metagenic virus. Their intent is to make sure any treatment doesn't harm the interests of Earth or the Klingon leadership. Reed finds the conflict of loyalties between Section 31 and his captain so difficult that he rejects an invitation to continue as a Section 31 operative.

In 2259 of the *Kelvin* Timeline, Section 31 has a huge, top-secret infrastructure. This includes a large underground facility in London, a starbase in orbit of Io, and a massive warship, the *Vengeance* (*Star Trek Into Darkness*). Admiral Marcus and other hawkish leaders might have developed all of this infrastructure entirely within the *Kelvin* Timeline (from 2233 forward). More likely, though, the secretive agency has developed significant resources during more than a hundred years in operation, so at least some of these facilities probably exist in the Prime Timeline as well.

In 2257, Section 31 recruits Emperor Georgiou to become an operative. No doubt they are impressed by her plan to end the war by destroying the Klingon homeworld.

Star Trek of that war or the suffering it caused. Is it possible to reverse-engineer a hypothetical in-universe reason for this? One theory might be that the Federation's leaders make the same decision about the war that they make about the Mirror Universe – to act, as much as possible, as if it didn't exist. They could have decided the quickest path to recovery would be to put the war entirely behind them. Honor the dead, but don't dwell on the losses or the events of the war. Instead, rebuild and move on, and look only to the future.

Ten years after the war, the Federation appears fully recovered, and already looking outward again.

If Federation and Starfleet leaders promoted such a policy widely across the Federation, silence – at least in public – about the war might become normal behavior in a relatively short time, just as civilians during World War II quickly learned to embrace challenging policies such as blackouts and rationing as patriotic behavior.

Successful pursuit of the rebuilding part of this policy could explain why, 10 years after the war, the Federation appears fully recovered, and already looking outward again – not with imperialist ambition like the Klingons, but with genuine scientific curiosity. The Five Year Mission is an expression of that recovery and a new confidence. You don't send your most powerful ship out to explore deep space unless you feel certain you won't need its military assets to defend your territory.

The Organian Factor

The Organian incident can also be seen in a new light thanks to the war. When Kirk and Kor come face to face in "Errand of Mercy," the war has been over for barely a decade. Both officers would have fought in it – where else but in that war could Kirk have gotten his reputation as a formidable enemy of the Klingons (*Star Trek VI: The Undiscovered Country*)? Kor's eagerness for another "glorious" war and his regret that the Organians put a stop to it could be put down to the Klingons' many victories during the previous war.

Kirk is also uncharacteristically militaristic on Organia, and seems so eager for war with the Klingons that he is surprised at himself afterward. In other confrontations with a hostile force (for example "The Corbomite Maneuver" and "Balance of Terror"), he is bold but doesn't fight until he has to. But here he finds himself facing the old enemy again, on the brink of another war. He might easily see this new Klingon aggression as a threat to be stopped here and now, at any cost.

We could also infer that the previous war is the reason the Organians decide to reveal themselves in 2267. They may have their own version of a "Prime Directive" that has kept them from interfering with lesser species before. When they see the same two "bad actors" from the last war getting ready to fight again, they decide they must intervene.

As *Discovery*'s second season develops, doubtless these questions of canon and continuity will be joined by fresh ones for fans to debate, as the gap to the original series continues to close. ⁘

11 General Chang greets Kirk as "one warrior to another" in *Star Trek VI: The Undiscovered Country*.

12 Section 31 agent (Mirror) Philippa Georgiou.

STAR TREK
DISCOVERY

BEING MICHAEL BURNHAM

Season 1 of *Star Trek: Discovery* put Michael Burnham through the wringer, propelling
the Vulcan-raised first officer from the depths of despair and disgrace to a redemptive
triumph by season's end. But as actor Sonequa Martin-Green reveals, Burnham's journey
of redemption is far from over, as she tries to find a balance between logic and emotion,
complicated by the arrival on *Discovery* of her adoptive brother, Spock.

Words: Ian Spelling

It was arguably the finest first-season moment
for both *Star Trek: Discovery* and its leading
lady, Sonequa Martin-Green. In the closing few
minutes of the season finale, "Will You Take
My Hand?", Martin-Green's Michael Burnham
delivered a remarkable speech, realized on
screen in part as a voiceover and in part with
Burnham at a ceremony, standing before her
fellow *U.S.S. Discovery* crew sporting their
Starfleet Medals of Honor, and a contingent of
applauding Starfleet officers.

Among Burnham's most stirring lines were
these examples:

"The only way to defeat fear is to tell it 'No.'
No, we will not take shortcuts on the path to
righteousness. No, we will not break the rules that
protect us from our basest instincts. No, we will
not allow desperation to destroy moral authority."

Burnham's oration served to close out much
of her unique arc. She began her journey as a
figure torn between her human nature and a
Vulcan upbringing, enduring a fraught relationship
with her father, Sarek (James Frain), whose own
choices were revealed to have haunted him
and his relationship with his daughter. Burnham

stepped aboard *Discovery* riddled with guilt over
her actions that led to the death of her mentor,
Captain Philippa Georgiou (Michelle Yeoh), and
her reputation preceded her: the crew didn't trust
her, especially at first. Captain Lorca (Jason Isaacs),
however, gave her a shot at redemption, even
though that gesture proved to be part of a devious
long game.

Ultimately, though, Burnham helped save the
day and end the war with the Klingons. She came
to make peace with Saru (Doug Jones) and Sarek,
forged a friendship with Tilly (Mary Wiseman), and
found love with Ash Tyler (Shazad Latif). And she
found herself looking forward – with a tear in her
eye and a smile on her face – to a future full of
promise and hope.

Redemption Song

"That speech, it's the end of the journey in Season
1, but it will resonate in Season 2, because it's not
over," the always-warm, emotional, and talkative
Martin-Green notes over the course of two
separate conversations. "It's just the beginning of
it, actually, because the redemption arc that we
explored in Season 1 continues.

01

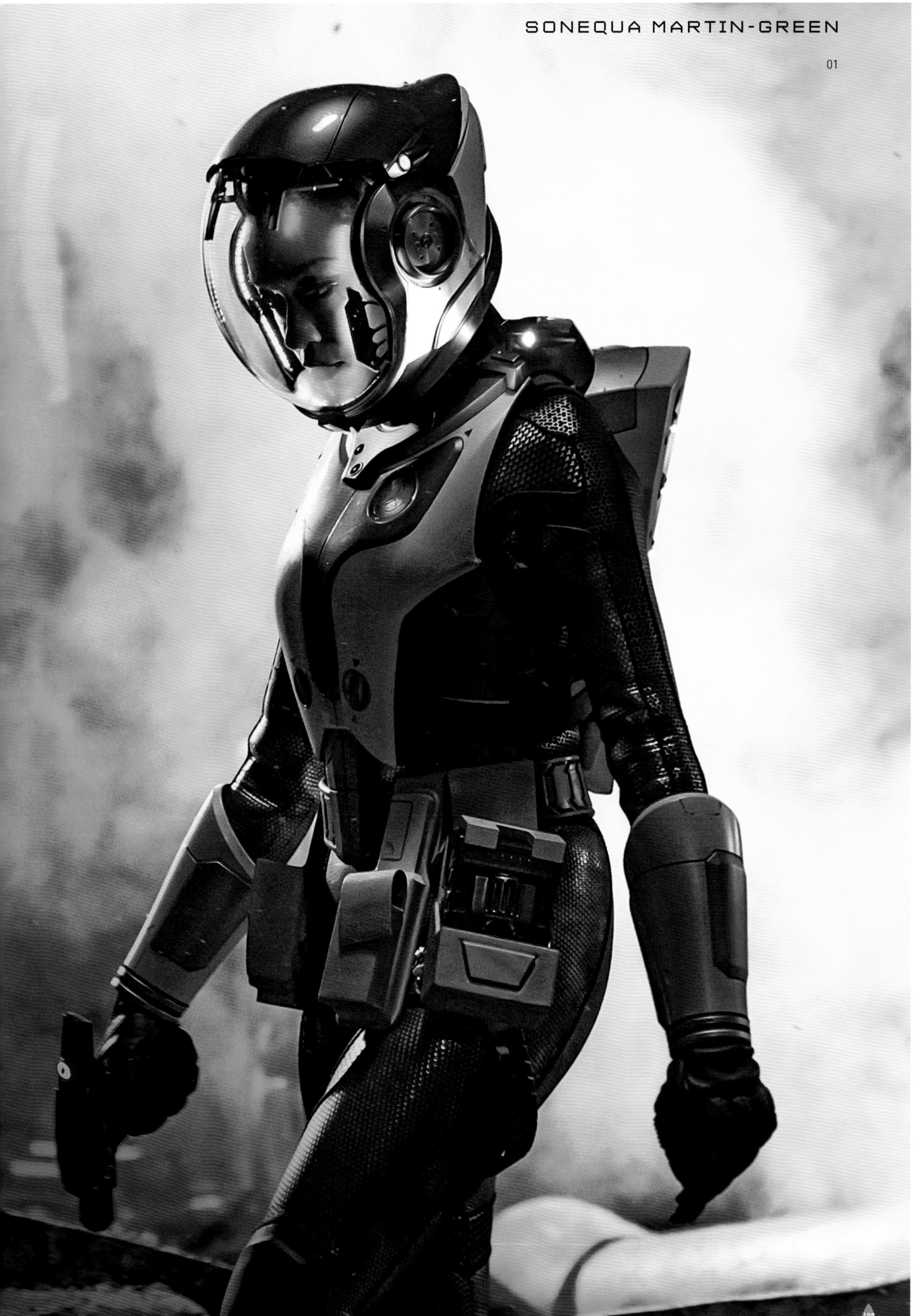

02

"There was certainly some professional redemption. There was the reinstatement into Starfleet. There was the interpersonal redemption. A lot of the people on the ship stopped looking at me like they wanted to kill me, and forgave me, and obviously my loved ones and whatnot. But what is most important is that Burnham forgives herself, because as Burnham, I carry a tremendous amount of guilt and shame. That's a foundation in my heart, unfortunately, because of the tragic event of my parents being murdered, and me essentially being responsible for that.

"So, that then factors into your very identity as a child, and you carry that for the rest of your life," the actress says. "It's going to be very important that I forgive myself and realize that it is not about me denying my emotions because of my logic training and upbringing, but it is also not about denying my logic so that I can fulfill my emotions.

"There's been a sort of waterfall happening, right? A sort of a bursting of the dam, if you will, because for so long it was so shut down and closed off, and then it just sort of opened up at the end of Episode 6 ["Lethe"] in Season 1,

01 A besuited Burnham strides through the wreckage of the *U.S.S. Hiawatha.*

02 Burnham side-by-side with (Prime) Georgiou in "Battle at the Binary Stars."

03 With Tyler in "Magic to Make the Sanest Man Go Mad."

04 Professional redemption in "Will You Take My Hand?"

05 Deceived by Lorca in "Despite Yourself."

"Burnham and Spock is a difficult, complicated relationship, and we dig into it very deeply."

and now it's just bursting and bursting and bursting. We're still there in that place, and at this point, now, I have to understand. I say to Sarek in the pilot that my emotions inform my logic. But now what I need to learn as Burnham is how my logic informs my emotions."

We Are Family

Martin-Green beams brightly when asked what she considered the biggest surprises during Season 1, so far as shooting *Discovery* and portraying Burnham. "I would say I think what was surprising to me was just how much it continued to unfold," she replies. "And how deep it went, and how inclusive this entire experience and community was going to be. And also just how close we as a company, with *Discovery*, became a family. That was also very surprising.

"Character-wise, I think I wouldn't say that anything was surprising in the sense that it shocked me or I disagreed with it, or I thought, 'Ooh, why is this happening this way?' Everything definitely made sense and tracked, and I think it was an organic progression. But it was definitely thrilling to go through the ups and downs and twists and turns."

Second Season Secrets

Season 2 of *Discovery* is underway now, having launched on January 17 in the US and Canada, and on January 18 elsewhere around the world. Even so, Martin-Green chooses her words carefully when addressing details of the show's sophomore year.

"Well, I think people expect the fallout from everything that happened last year," she says. "There's so many things that happened. So many decisions were made. So many changes happened. There was evolution in Season 1, but we weren't able to dig into it because we were at war. So, you will see all of that. You will see people dealing with what's left. Dealing with the residual [effects], dealing with, 'Okay, what do I have now? What have

I done? What does that mean? Who am I? Who are we?' You'll see people asking those questions and seeking to answer them in Season 2.

"And there is a lot more… there's a little more joy just because we aren't at war," she continues. "We're able to smile a little bit more. There's a sense of levity that's there simply because we're not fighting for our lives. There's certainly a heaviness that is present with me as Burnham, just because of everything that is driving me and because there are

"A crew is almost defined by the essence of the captain. We went through the ringer with Lorca, and so there's a little bit of PTSD there."

deep-seated problems there. So, those are still at play, for sure. But yes, you see the smile, and you see the chuckles that we allow ourselves to have, including Burnham, because we're not fighting."

Evolving Relationships

Martin-Green goes on to tease how Burnham's relationships will continue to evolve. Chief among them is Tyler, the physically and emotionally broken man with whom she fell in love. They'd amicably moved on from each other at

06

07

Sonequa Martin-Green on Fandom

Sonequa Martin-Green arrived at *Star Trek: Discovery* following several years playing Sasha Williams on *The Walking Dead*. That franchise, like *Star Trek*, boasts a massive, passionate, and devoted fan base. The common denominator between the franchises, Martin-Green believes, is the devotion of the fans.

"That's the similarity, right?" she argues. "I find that that's the case with sci-fi in general, and it has made me come to dearly love and respect sci-fi for that reason. I mean, I've always loved sci-fi, as a child and as a teenager and whatnot, but now I really understand its power. It's because of these fantastic circumstances, right? These hyper-realities that we get to live in that open up our hearts, and help us suspend our disbelief, and then, all the themes that are there. The themes of truth and love and diversity and universality just come right in. They just flood right in, and you don't even readily realize what's happening.

"That's what I love about sci-fi, and so that is reflected in the fan base," Martin-Green concludes. "I can't love these people more because I truly believe it is a collective communion that we're all in together. We're all having this shared experience over this thing that is bigger than us. So, I love it."

the end of Season 1, but their feelings clearly lingered. The same, though, could be said of Tyler-Voq's bond with the formidable Klingon, L'Rell (Mary Chieffo), perhaps setting the stage for a love triangle.

"That was a unique experience for Burnham," Martin-Green says. "I had never been in love before, as Michael Burnham. That was the very first love situation, a very new thing to go to a loving relationship from the upbringing that I had. And yes, this concept of love, I'm still learning about it, and still understanding, especially because the self-love is something I'm still trying to learn. And Burnham actually may not be even completely conscious, may not even be completely aware of that self-love and how hard it really is to do it. And that is the key. I'm just saying. I just know as Sonequa, that that's what needs to happen."

Husband on Board

Speaking of love, *Discovery's* second season will feature a particularly unique guest star: Kenric Green, Martin-Green's husband and the father of her son, Kenric Justin Green II. Grinning happily and proudly, Martin-Green shares her enthusiasm about working with her spouse, but keeps mum about his role and the number of episodes in which he'll appear.

06 Rebuilding bridges with Saru in "Choose Your Pain."

07 On stage with Ethan Peck and Michelle Yeoh at New York Comic-Con.

08 Burnham on EVA in Season 2.

"I cannot say anything at all about that," she explains. "I can say that he will play a very memorable role, but he's just a brilliant actor, and caught the eye of the producers and casting directors. There came the perfect role for him, and he won it and he got it, and here we are. It's amazing. I'm very excited for everyone to see what he can do, and to see his soul and his spirit because he's such a powerful person, and such a beautiful person, and is that as well as an artist."

Have the two of them ever worked together before?

"We actually did," Martin-Green responds. "We worked together, sort of, on *The Walking Dead*. We were only in one scene together. We didn't speak to each other, but we were in the scene together. But then, before that, we were in a play together [*Fetch Clay, Make Man*], in Princeton, New Jersey, of all places, at the McCarter Theatre, and that is actually where we met."

(New) Captain on the Bridge

Moving on to other second-season developments and relationships, there's Captain Christopher Pike (Anson Mount) to consider. His entrance sets in motion all manner of on-board drama. Remember, Saru was last seen settling into the captain's chair as acting captain. Burnham is no doubt on the fast track to that same seat. And the last guy in the chair, Lorca, he of the Mirror Universe, wreaked tremendous havoc and deceived and betrayed his entire crew for far too long.

"I say to Sarek in the pilot that my emotions inform my logic. But now what I need to learn as Burnham is how my logic informs my emotions."

10

"A crew is almost defined by the essence of the captain," Martin-Green observes. "We went through the wringer with Lorca, and so there's a little bit of PTSD there. There's a little bit of distrust there because of what we've gone through and because we had someone who manipulated us and sought to kill us for his own gain. And so, Pike being the deeply rooted good guy he is, he is going to have an effect on us. He's soothing in that way. He's comforting in that way. Hopefully, you will see us sort of galvanize because of that.

"And I love Anson," the actress adds. "I just think he's awesome, and he's such an amazing actor. I feel like we really lose ourselves in the story together, which is amazing. Chemistry is something that is hard to know, as an actor, when you're in the middle of it; it's hard to say, 'Do we have chemistry?' I can feel what I feel, but other people are the ones to tell you if there's chemistry there. And so, we were very delighted to hear that people see chemistry between us, and I think that it's a great relationship because he's a great guy and we love having him."

Finally, the other major new relationship that will be explored this season is the one between Burnham and Spock (Ethan Peck). Not surprisingly, Martin-Green offers just a few words on the subject. "It is a difficult relationship," she says. "I can tell you that. It is a difficult, complicated relationship, and we dig into it very deeply. I really love it, and I'm very excited for you to see it." ✦

09 Shocked by red signals.

10 Live long and prosper.

EPISODE GUIDE
SEASON 2

EPISODE 1
"BROTHER"
The *U.S.S. Discovery* receives a distress call from the *U.S.S. Enterprise*. Her captain, Christopher Pike, takes command of *Discovery* and explains that he is investigating seven mysterious red signals. Subsequently, Commander Burnham experiences a vision of a red figure, and learns that Spock, who is on leave from the *Enterprise*, had knowledge of the signals.

EPISODE 2
"NEW EDEN"
Discovery detects one of the red signals, leading the ship to a planet whose human population hails from Earth circa World War III. After averting a disaster, Pike and *Discovery* learn that the planet's residents were transported there by the Red Angel from Burnham's vision.

EPISODE 3
"POINT OF LIGHT"
Spock escapes from the psychiatric unit he has committed himself to, seemingly killing three doctors in the process. Elsewhere, Tyler is recruited by the former Emperor Georgiou into covert Starfleet intelligence outfit Section 31.

EPISODE 4
"AN OBOL FOR CHARON"
Discovery is immobilized by a huge living Sphere, containing incredible amounts of information from all over the galaxy, which it wishes to transmit before it dies. Meanwhile, Ensign Sylvia Tilly is consumed by a parasite that claims *Discovery* is destroying its mycelial ecosystem.

EPISODE 5
"SAINTS OF IMPERFECTION"
Tilly has been taken into the mycelial network in order to stop a "monster" that is ravaging it. Following her, Burnham and Stamets discover that the "monster" is Doctor Culber, Stamets' lover; his body is rebuilt in the real world, returning him to life.

EPISODE 6
"THE SOUND OF THUNDER"
Following a red signal to Saru's homeworld, Pike and *Discovery* find a society where Saru's species,

the Kelpiens, are hunted by a predator species, the Ba'ul. After Pike tries to forge a peace between the two species, the Red Angel appears and prevents the Ba'ul from retaliating.

EPISODE 7
"LIGHT AND SHADOWS"
While Pike and Tyler combat a time anomaly – one that secretly infects Lieutenant Commander Airiam – Burnham visits Vulcan, where she finds Spock. Instructed by Sarek to turn him over to Section 31 so they can mend his mind, she instead escapes with him, aided by Georgiou.

EPISODE 8
"IF MEMORY SERVES"
Burnham and Spock travel to Talos IV, where the Talosians heal Spock's mind. After Spock reveals that the Red Angel is a time traveler trying to prevent a catastrophe, the pair are retrieved by *Discovery*, whose crew, as a result, are now fugitives from Starfleet.

EPISODE 9
"PROJECT DAEDALUS"
After it's revealed that the footage of Spock murdering his doctors was faked, Admiral Cornwell directs *Discovery* to Section 31 HQ, where they find Section 31's AI, Control, has killed all personnel on board. Using Airiam as its agent, Control attempts to obtain the database *Discovery* inherited from the Sphere, resulting in Airiam's death.

EPISODE 10
"THE RED ANGEL"
Burnham learns that the Red Angel is a time travel suit built by her real parents, ultimately leading to their deaths. Using Burnham as bait, *Discovery* and Section 31 operative Leland lure the Red Angel into a trap, unmasking the traveler as Burnham's mother.

EPISODE 11
"PERPETUAL INFINITY"
Burnham's mother reveals that she has traveled back 950 years from a future where all sentient life has been destroyed by Control. To prevent Control from obtaining the Sphere data, *Discovery*'s crew plan to upload it into the time suit, but Leland, now possessed by Control, intercepts the data and escapes with half of it.

EPISODE 12
"THROUGH THE VALLEY OF SHADOWS"
Tracking a red signal to a Klingon monastery whose monks guard time crystals, Pike retrieves a crystal, in the process experiencing a vision of his future self disabled in an accident. Back on *Discovery*, the ship is besieged by a Section 31 fleet under the command of Control.

EPISODE 13
"SUCH SWEET SORROW, PART 1"
After rendezvousing with the *Enterprise*, Burnham devises a plan to use the time crystal to take *Discovery* and the Sphere data into the far future, out of Control's reach. Pike resumes command of the *Enterprise* to keep Control busy while *Discovery* makes her escape.

EPISODE 14
"SUCH SWEET SORROW, PART 2"
The *Enterprise* and a Klingon fleet commanded by L'Rell fend off Control's forces, allowing Burnham to travel to the past in the time suit to place the red signals that brought everyone to this point, then lead *Discovery* over 900 years into an unknown future. Pike, Spock, and the *Enterprise* crew report that *Discovery* was destroyed in the battle with Control.

STAR TREK
DISCOVERY

THE *DISCO* SET

Late in 2018, during a break in filming for *Star Trek: Discovery* Season 2, *Star Trek Magazine* beamed aboard the *U.S.S. Discovery* – or rather, the Toronto soundstages that house it – to find out what's changed on the ship this season, and what we should be watching for in the revamped sets.

Words: Darren Scott

THE BRIDGE

Our tour guide is Jody Clement, one of three art directors on the series. We arrive at the first of the many huge stages utilized for the show, the bridge. The set looms above us, as it's raised up from the floor. Naturally, there's no actual viewscreen in there, so we're able to see the set fully lit within. Before we take the wooden steps up to the set, there are sticky mats outside the entrance to prevent dirt and grit from getting into filming areas.

Entering at the front, from the left side of the viewscreen, it's impossible not to let out a cry of excitement to be standing on the bridge of the *Discovery*. Jody points out that many people assume the see-through screens are all operated by visual effects. "It's a surprise for a lot of people when they arrive on set to see these fantastic organic LED screens," she comments; they are all programmed on computer by "an amazing graphic animation department that makes sure that every screen you see on the bridge, in the corridors, in all of our sets are unique screens. There is minimal repetition. Every screen on the bridge will be different."

As you might expect, when looking at the viewscreen, the cast will be looking at a big green screen that is pulled across the soundstage. Jody explains that a monitor is set up so the cast can see whatever strange new encounter they're having. "It may be in the early concept stage, but it gives them a general idea so they're not all guessing at what the planet or spaceship looks like. That makes it a little easier for them."

We walk across the circular set, surprised to hear the sounds of feet on wooden floors rather than metal. Such is the magic of television... "This set was upwards of three-and-a-half to four months to build," Jody tells us.

SCIENCE LAB

A new addition to the set for Season 2, the science lab is located behind the bridge. Designed to be a research area, this is the ready room refitted – which, Jody notes, is a story point that she can't go into. The lab has a lot of plants in a small area that is divided off with a glass wall. On screens you can see the quantum physics lab. There are what appears to be spores or geological rocks in suspended animation, hanging in the air, set into the walls, and petri dishes with blue and yellow liquid and some small, caterpillar-like creatures. Jody points out that, thanks to the set dressers, there are vegetable steamers in the walls that are all lit up. "They'll find a use for almost everything out there."

READY ROOM

But where's the ready room? "The captain's ready room, in relation to the bridge now, is half a deck up through the turbo lifts," Jody tells us. And yes, they do keep the actual geography of the ship in mind when undertaking changes.

Sadly we don't get to see this new area, but Jody says it took 8 to 10 weeks to build. "It's smaller, so it doesn't have the scope, but definitely carrying on some of the details that we have on the *Discovery* bridge." Jody also reveals that Anson Mount (Captain Pike) was involved with the design, and that Production Designer Tamara Deverell had a conversation with him about what she felt Pike would have in his room in terms of decoration – something that previously happened with Michelle Yeoh and Georgiou's ready room for the *U.S.S. Shenzhou*.

> ## Yes, of course we take the opportunity to sit in the captain's chair. Yes, of course we gasp.

THE CAPTAIN'S CHAIR... AND BEYOND

Yes, of course we take the opportunity to sit in the captain's chair. Yes, of course we gasp. You can push the buttons on the arms and the panels go up. The left-hand arm has communications and phasers, while the right has alerts, shields, and a variety of torpedo options. We press carefully. And although the chair does spin, we're asked not to – many people have pulled the wires out from underneath while doing so!

"We took Anson Mount for a tour and said, 'Would you like me to take a photo of you in the captain's chair?'" reports Jody. "He got very emotional!"

There's a *U.S.S. Discovery* plaque located on the wall behind the chair, which Jody points out houses a little Easter egg: "The names along the silver band at the bottom are members of the production team." Jody takes us to the rear right of the captain's chair. "Last season, over in the

03

corner, we had blue control lights all in the wall. We decided to give the set a little more interest by removing this wall, and repurposed these elements. We used to call this corner HAL, as a nod to *2001: A Space Odyssey*. We opened it up and it allows for crew members to enter the set from something other than the turbo lift or the old ready room.

"It's a process, discovering things throughout the course of the season," Jody says, mentioning that things have moved to allow for the sight lines of actors. "That area with HAL was considered a bit dark in the background and didn't have any life to it, so that was a decision to give it life."

TURBOLIFT AND DOORS

The turbolift is clearly labeled as "deck one bridge" and has 17 other decks, with additional options for sounding an alarm or heading to the airlock. And having always wondered if the swishing doors on *Star Trek* are worked by motion sensors, Jody's here to set us straight: "Our special effects operator will open the door by the open/close buttons that are there, but we have cameras on the other side of the doors so that when an actor approaches, they will push the button and the doors will open. We do have bloopers of doors not opening…"

01 Ace *Star Trek Magazine* reporter Darren Scott takes the opportunity to try out the *Discovery* captain's chair.

02 Don't touch that, Darren!

03 One to beam down.

04 Darren poses for a memento of his visit to the *Crossfield*-class starship.

It's a brilliant feeling simply to walk along the corridors of the *Discovery*.

ENGINEERING

There are further steps up to engineering, as, once inside the entrance, there are metal steps going down into what is quite a high set.

"One of the changes that we did this year was that we opened up engineering a bit more," Jody says, guiding us to the wall on the left and a track on either side of the set. "In our *Star Trek* world, the door raises up – and that would be on both sides; it's a blast shield door and right behind there is the dilithium chamber. You can see a series of pipes, and then we have a backdrop just beyond those pipes to give the illusion that the dilithium chamber goes a lot further."

Jody estimates it increases the size of the set by half, thanks to three huge panel backdrops that have been included. "It's mostly background, but you can shoot more. The idea was it just felt a little close so we opened it out for better shooting angles."

SHUTTLE BAY

Housed in the largest purpose-built

soundstage in North America, measuring 46,000 square feet, with a height of 60 feet, the shuttle bay is actually only a small section. Simply put, they can't build any more of it. "The shuttle bay would be as high as the ceiling in the stage here, so 60 feet, with two more bays – one on either side," Jody explains, estimating that only a sixth of the area exists in real life.

CORRIDOR HUBS

Jody next takes us to one of the corridor hubs. Taking apart various bits of the panels, she divulges that the sets were originally created for the *Shenzhou*.

"We didn't have time to build a whole new set of corridors, so this set was designed to be modular – so the bumpers come off, new bumpers go on, another part comes off, and then behind it you'll see the *Shenzhou* design." As we walk these now legendary corridors, Jody points out the letters "GNDN" – as seen in the original series – on various pipes. What does it mean? "Goes Nowhere, Does Nothing," of course!

The corridors now have a new extended area, which Jody notes was previously the airlock. "We do have the ability to change it back into the airlock as and when we need it, but one of the things we found last year was that directors were finding it difficult

to stage a scene with a continuous walk and talk. So this year we can do a continuous loop as many times as we want. We opened this set up – the airlock has gone away, we've actually made the ceilings a little higher. We call it more of a mechanical corridor, as if it's going to the engineering section. We have some green screen up above, not to space, but more of the pipes and the things that you see on the walls, raised up on various levels in the ship."

We walk past ladders and doors. These also go nowhere and do nothing, but with the continuation of the corridor sets, they now snake on and on. It's a brilliant feeling simply to walk along the corridors of the *Discovery*.

MESS HALL

"The mess hall last season looked a little different," Jody tells us. "It had a completely different entrance. What we used to do was change over the mess hall into crew quarters and back into the mess hall. That was a challenge for us on many levels. It also had a lot of wear and tear on the set when we were changing it over; the lights would be pulled out, we'd have to repair them. So this season we decided to make a permanent crew quarters on the other side of the wall, and we extended the mess hall the equal amount that we

lost from the crew quarters. But what happened was that we lost the original entrance, so we made a second entrance. So it's the mess hall on deck five instead of the mess hall on deck two!"

TRANSPORTER ROOM

On to the transporter room. Once you've let it sink in that you're actually standing on a real transporter pad, there are touch screens that work. "There are some on the bridge, I believe there's one at Saru's station," Jody says. "But it was very important that these were touch screens for this set." She encourages us to touch one and operate the transporters.

Once again, this set was also originally built for the *Shenzhou*. A platform in the center was added, and three of the pads removed to make the set "snugger." "We can change the colors of the lights, and we have a little flicker effect that will signal the transport happening, and then the visual effects people take over."

Jody points out that, underneath the reinforced glass on the floor, there are handles from ice scrapers built into the design.

"On most TV shows, the set decorators and set dressers go and buy appliances, furniture, and office equipment. We don't really have that on this show, so all of the pipes and the things that you see in the floor, we have an entire team in a building adjacent to this property; they just spend their time building things to go into the floors, into the walls. They will go and buy water bottles that have the inserts you

put fruit in – if you look around, you'll find them."

CREW QUARTERS

As we make our way into a junior crew quarter – which Jody reveals was a section of the mess hall from last season – we take a well-earned rest on the single bed. It's a nice, firm mattress – just what you need in space.

Jody explains that they can expand the quarters as rank determines, adding in a bathroom or extra walls. Outside the windows, as you might expect, there are green screens.

SICKBAY

Our last stop is sickbay – but not as we know it!

"We have multiple sickbays," Jody tells us. "In fact, we make reference to being in a different sickbay a couple of times this season. When you watch the season, you'll see sickbay will change up. It's the same sickbay, we just make a few changes. New to this season is a medical synthesizer so the doctors can synthesize any kind of medication they need."

She picks up two small metal items and smiles. "In the original series, Bones used salt and pepper shakers almost exactly like this to scan. If you can see, there is a 'P' there: it is a pepper shaker, so that's a nod to the original series."

And as for those futuristic beds? "These are regular gurneys that we've clad with Starfleet Medical graphics. We built a whole unit to fit over the top of an existing gurney. We painted them a little differently for a different ship," she adds, enigmatically. ★

04

STAR TREK
DISCOVERY

EXECUTIVE
SUMMARY

With brand new episodes of *Star Trek: Discovery* debuting on CBS All Access and Netflix, *Star Trek: Magazine* explores the secrets of Season 2 with Executive Producer Heather Kadin and fellow EP – and now showrunner – Alex Kurtzman. And as the pair reveal, many of those secrets take the form of the untold story of Burnham and Spock…

Words: Mark Newbold

Star Trek Magazine: Alex, what can you tell us about the second season of *Star Trek: Discovery* that you've never revealed before?
Alex Kurtzman: We are going to sync up with canon at the end of the season.

And Heather, could you reveal something?
Heath Kadin: Something's going to change about Saru. *(Laughs)* There could be a lot of changes emotionally.

Season 1 of *Discovery* introduced the characters and laid out the perils for the crew. Moving into the second year, what has been the trickiest aspect so far?
AK: Well, obviously there's a lot of questions from last season, right? How come Spock never mentioned his half-sister Michael Burnham? We owe the audience an answer to that.

One of the things that I'm the most excited about this season is that this is the untold chapter of Spock. This is Spock pre-the original series. He's not actualized as the character

you know from the original series yet. He has seen something that his logical brain and logical training cannot make sense of, and he is emotionally ill-equipped to deal with it. So, logic and emotion have failed Spock, and he is trying to figure out who he is and what the red signal means and what the red angel means. And it is through his relationship, his very complicated and broken relationship with Michael, that he is able to actualize himself as the Spock we know from the original series, and that's a big part of what the season's about.

With the changes in the writers' room during the first season, how have you managed to keep everything lined up in regards to the wider story?
AK: Because we've never really left the process of story breaking, and I was there very much through the beginning of Season 2, so when the shift happened it was a natural progression. We didn't invent anything new at that point, we just kept the plan that we already had.

Section 31, first introduced in *Star Trek: Deep Space Nine* and expanded upon in *Star Trek: Enterprise* and *Star Trek Into Darkness*, is back. What attracts you to this shadowy organization?

AK: Starfleet lives in a very black-and-white world. They have rules, they have to stick to those rules. You can bend them, but you can't break them. Section 31 lives entirely in shades of gray and they do all of the things that Starfleet proper can't do. That's really interesting, because when you have a character like Georgiou, whose conscience is constantly being tested and her ethics are constantly being tested, she's really in some ways the perfect person to do the dirty work *(laughs)* that Starfleet can't do. That's an exciting place to explore. It's a little bit gloves off, which is what's exciting about Section 31.

> ## "Georgiou is in some ways the perfect person to do the dirty work that Starfleet can't do."
> ### ALEX KURTZMAN

Was it your intention from the very beginning to have Georgiou join Section 31?

AK: Yes. It actually evolved halfway through the [first] season. The plan from the beginning was to kill her in the second episode [in order] to bring her back in the Mirror Universe; and then, when we were thinking about how we wanted to set up the second season and where we wanted to go, it made a lot of logical sense that she would become part of Section 31.

Season 1 of *Discovery* focused on our new crew of characters, and for large parts of the season they were separated from the rest of Starfleet. What made you decide to bring in more Starfleet characters, specifically the legendary Captain Pike and "The Cage"-era crew?

HK: A lot of it started with the fact that we owed the explanation about Spock to Burnham, so how best to sync up with that story? We felt bringing Pike in to be our introduction to the original series was the best way to go, especially

02

01 Burnham, Linus, and Saru share a turbolift with Pike and the *Enterprise* crew.

02 Philippa Georgiou returns.

03 Number One – Rebecca Romijn – makes her entrance.

04 Ethan Peck as Spock.

05 Kurtzman and Kadin on stage at NYCC.

with Lorca leaving. There was a chair absent, so to speak, so that was a big factor.

Was it always the case that Spock would be involved in *Discovery* in a deeper way than merely being name-checked as Burnham's "brother"?

AK: Early on, we knew we wanted to do it, but we also knew we had to cast appropriately, and we had to come up with a version of Spock that we hadn't seen before – not a negation of what we'd seen before, which is a different version. I love that this part of Spock is just a part of his life that you've never seen. Finding Ethan [Peck] was a search.

It took a while, so we didn't want to put too much information out there until we understood how we wanted to present it.

To paraphrase Valeris in *Star Trek VI: The Undiscovered Country*, Leonard Nimoy could only be succeeded, never replaced. Given that, and the timeframe in which *Discovery* is set, what were you looking for in your search for Spock?

HK: I think because of the time of Spock's life we're going to be looking into and diving into, we wanted someone who exhibited those qualities that you've seen in the later versions of Spock, but also he's younger, so on one

hand you can't have someone who's completely youthful and vulnerable. It's like casting a younger version of yourself. It's hard because you want that person to look like they could grow into the person you know, so that's kind of hard to find.

AK: I think also there's a misconception that Vulcans don't have emotion. A lot of people think that, but that's not the case at all. They contain it very differently than humans do, so what you're looking for from an actor is someone who can convey an enormous amount of emotion behind that stoic Vulcan veneer. When Ethan came in and

read, it was really, really clear that he was feeling so much, and working so hard to contain it. Especially with the Spock that you're going to see this season, who doesn't know what to do with his emotions and doesn't understand how logic and emotion fit together yet. He just seemed like the guy. It was just very natural.

It does read that Spock learns more about how to be a Vulcan from Michael, a human, than he does from his own people.
AK: Well, it's funny, we pitched this season in some ways as, this is the season about a human who learns

emotion from a Vulcan, and a Vulcan who learns logic from a human. So it was an interesting barometer for how we wanted to gauge our relationship between the brother and the sister.

HK: But also we had to earn that. You had to see Burnham go through her own journey last season of shedding a lot of her Vulcan ways, which is also what makes her human teaching with Spock so beautiful.

While we only saw her once, played by Majel Barrett in the original pilot from 1965, Number One is a unique and important character. How will she be fleshed out in Season 2?

THAT PICARD SHOW

Star Trek Magazine: You have two live action shows in production at the moment – *Star Trek: Discovery* and the Jean-Luc Picard series. Is there much overlap in the production and development of the two shows?

Alex Kurtzman: Right now they're very separate, entirely separate shows.

Heather Kadin: What we can say about that show – and I think any shows that we're going to be doing in this universe – is that they should all feel of a different voice from one another, and they should feel like you're having a different viewing experience. When we were first meeting with Patrick Stewart, it was very important to him that it wasn't just like you're watching another *Discovery* – that the Picard show feels very different, and the way we're going to shoot it is going to look different, and the way we're going to tell the stories is going to be different; and that's going to be a conscious choice with anything else we do.

We're about to meet Jean-Luc after almost 20 years. Thankfully the rest of the *Star Trek: The Next Generation* cast are all fit and healthy. Could we be seeing an *Enterprise*-E reunion at some point?

AK: There have been many conversations about many things.

07

06

AK: It's interesting, because there's so little that you know about Number One – which is great, because she's kind of a blank canvas – but here's what you do know. She's clearly very competent, she's very strong, [Captain Pike] relies on her tremendously, she knows what she's doing, and we built all of that into our version of Number One. The other thing we added is that she's extremely resourceful, meaning that she knows how to work the system in order to get what she needs for her ship and her crew. In some ways, while she's not the captain, we think of her as one because she's very strong. You'll see a lot of that, and what Rebecca [Romijn] brings to it.

Season 1 of *Discovery* brought us the first F-bomb in *Star Trek* history. What freedom do you have on a digital platform like CBS All Access, as opposed to a regular TV network?
HK: In doing that, it was a conscious choice, natural to the moment and natural to the character. But it was something we talked about really early on – in the nascent stages with CBS All Access, even – and we all decided only if it's natural for the show, because you don't want to all of a sudden go to *Star Trek* and everyone's naked and having sex all over the place; it would look ridiculous. It's been a very conscious choice, even though we have the freedom to use it when it feels right for the show.

AK: I think also there was a lot of conversation about using the F-bomb and how. We used it as an expression of joy for science, so it felt very *Trek*

to do it that way, especially from a character who in so many ways is such an open heart. She just can't contain herself, she's so excited about what she's seeing, and it just pops out. That's very different than using it towards somebody, or in the context of being angry. That would feel a lot less joyful. And so, as with all things in *Trek*, it's always how do you play around with expectation without violating what is essential about *Star Trek*.

Will there be more F-bombs in Season 2?
AK: Not so far.

Discovery has been heralded for its ever-broadening range of diversity. Is that something that you intend to continue expanding throughout the second season and beyond?
AK: I think diversity is an essential tenet of *Trek*. The greatest contribution of Roddenberry's vision was that diversity was an assumption. Nobody talked about it because it just was. Gender parity was an assumption, and I think, *Trek* being a mirror to the world that we live in, it's more timely than ever to be able to tell those stories, to embed them in every choice we make on *Trek*.

The *Discovery* sets are movie-quality in size, scope, and scale. Bringing in such an iconic location as the bridge of the *U.S.S. Enterprise* takes the show up to the next level in terms of ambition and public awareness. How does it feel to be involved with the creation of a new *Enterprise* set?

> ## "We are going to sync up with canon at the end of the season."
> ### ALEX KURTZMAN

Star Trek. When you walk around and you see the level of detail that the production designers have given everything, from the consoles to the chairs to the layout, these are things that we sweat over.

Has the *Enterprise* been given a 2019 refresh, or is it recognizably the bridge of the *Enterprise* that we remember from "The Cage"?
AK: It will look different from the *Kelvin Enterprise*. Without giving away too much, I think we are doing what we do in all of *Discovery*, which is, what is the essential spirit of what people loved about the things in the original series, and yet how do we make it look like it exists on our show? ⬩

AK: So, it's amazing. I had the incredible privilege of working on the movies where we had an *Enterprise* set, and it's a slightly different *Enterprise* set, because we're in the *Kelvin* Timeline. The look is different, but it's pretty amazing. People don't walk on to any of our bridges without stopping for

a minute and looking around. When Anson [Mount] first took the chair on *Discovery*, he was like, "I need a minute." He sat and it was a huge moment for him, and he got very emotional because it's like the fulfilment of a childhood dream, so it's wonderful to be on those bridges and it is essential

06 Patrick Stewart.

07 Culber and Stamets.

08 Tilly in "Runaway."

09 The *Kelvin Enterprise*.

LOVING THE ALIEN

From the Pale Man in *Pan's Labyrinth* to the Amphibian Man in *The Shape of Water*, Doug Jones has portrayed numerous memorable monsters, bringing him both creative fulfilment and fan acclaim. But the love he has for his *Star Trek: Discovery* character, Saru, and the love he has experienced from *Star Trek*'s fans, have been something else altogether. As *Discovery* Season 2 reaches its climax, Doug Jones divulges his passion for Saru and *Star Trek*.

WORDS: IAN SPELLING

Doug Jones has said goodbye twice now to Saru: first when Season 1 of *Star Trek: Discovery* wrapped, and again following the completion of Season 2. Each time it's been such sweet sorrow… for the most part.

"Well, I sort of have to let him go," Jones says. "That's part of the job. It's like leaving your best friends when you're off for the summer, back in our school days, right? So, it's, 'Bye everybody, see you in the fall!' The love doesn't go away, so you miss them – and that's good.

"Now, the make-up process… I don't miss that all the time. But the character, I do. I love him dearly and I miss him. Knowing that most likely he'll be back helps, too."

Though there are no guarantees in Hollywood, chances are neither Jones nor our Kelpien friend are going anywhere, ever. Jones, after all, is the veteran amongst the *Discovery* cast and beloved by his co-stars and the show's makers, who consider him an absolute pro, a particular blessing considering the actor's extensive, exhaustive daily make-up process.

CPM-660

01

Then there's Saru, who ranks up there with Sonequa Martin-Green's Michael Burnham and Mary Wiseman's Sylvia Tilly as one of the show's breakout characters. A scaredy-cat who's also courageous and ambitious, not to mention wise and occasionally funny…? Saru fits – and enhances – any scene with any character.

KNOWING ME, KNOWING SARU

Looking back on whatever expectations he harbored about Saru heading into Season 1, Jones reveals that the writers' room gave him and his co-stars an option: "How much do you want to know ahead?" Jones chose to hear just a little – or rather, just enough. "I'm one of those types that I want to get the new script for the next episode and be surprised," he explains. "I love a story to unfold as it unfolds, without knowing too much ahead.

"Now, I do need to know certain things, like what is a backstory to me that will be revealed later that I need to play now? That's the only thing I really needed to know. But as far as plot twists, and where we're all headed? When I came into the series as third in command, as the chief science officer on the starship *Shenzhou*, I really didn't know much about what happened beyond that.

"I knew that the *Shenzhou* would last for those first two episodes and that we would make the transition to the starship *Discovery*," the actor continues. "But as far as me being promoted to first officer, and what journey was ahead with *Discovery*, I really didn't know too much about that. So, I've been surprised every episode as I read it, kind of like watching the show as a fan would."

EMBRACING THE FANS

As for those fans, Jones can't thank them enough for their support – literally: anyone who has ever glimpsed him at a convention, *Star Trek* or otherwise, will be able to confirm that his autograph lines tend to be the longest. In part that's because he makes a genuinely profound connection with

02

03

people, speaking with them – not at or to them – and frequently standing up and walking around his table to envelop folks in what's come to be known as a "Doug Hug."

"This has been an absolute dream for me, just a delight," he says of his connection with the *Trek* faithful. "You never know. In a 32-year career, every role that I take on, you hope that this is the one that's going to hit. Over those 32 years, I've had several hits, but I've also had several that kind of fell off and were never remembered again. So, you just never know.

"I will say that the *Star Trek* conventions, specifically the ones in Las Vegas and Birmingham, the two that I've been to now, that's when you can have face time with these fans who are devoted to not just our series, but the entire franchise, and have been for their lifetime. The comment that I hear the most, that I just love hearing, is 'Welcome to the family.' That is

something that I didn't expect. I didn't even know about that. I did not know what a family feeling the *Star Trek* fandom had.

"So, to be embraced, and to have my character embraced, and to have so many people tell me, 'Saru is my favorite character on the show,' it's wonderful," he says. "I also hear, 'I really like Saru because I'm dealing with fear issues of my own. I have anxiety. I actually am in therapy now for my fears and my anxieties, and Saru really does help inspire and help motivate me to make it through the next day.' Hearing comments like that really warms my heart and makes me feel like I'm doing more than just an acting gig. It's actually something helpful for all of us.

"I deal with fear issues of my own," Jones continues. "I always have. Even when I get a new script for the next episode, I'm always terrified that I'm going to fail while playing it. So, I can learn from watching Saru and

01 Doug Jones as Saru in the *Short Treks* installment "The Brightest Star."

02 Saru encounters the Kelpien predators the Ba'ul, in Season 2, Episode 6, "The Sound of Thunder."

03 With sister Siranna, in "The Sound of Thunder"...

04 ...and with Burnham, Pike, and Tyler, in the same episode.

from being him that you can push your threat ganglia back in. You can forge ahead. Whatever we're afraid of, if we can step back from it and look at it, we might realize that there was nothing to be afraid of in the first place. And we learn that through Season 2 even more so with Saru."

SARU'S STAR

Saru's path to Season 2 included a unique detour, named "The Brightest Star." An installment of *Star Trek: Short Treks*, it centers on a much younger version of the Kelpien – though still played by Jones – on his home planet of Kaminar. The short also introduces his priest father (Robert Verlaque) and sister, Siranna (Hannah Spear), and fills in numerous blanks about Saru, with spillover carrying into Season 2. For example, Saru mentions his sibling issues during a conversation with Michael Burnham in "Brother," the second-season opener.

"Throughout Season 1, you see and hear Saru give many hints of his backstory, and where he comes from, that his home planet and his people are a prey species, and that we were herded and maybe farmed," Jones notes. "There was kind of a cattle reference, almost, it seemed. Your curiosities of where I come from are satisfied now with 'The Brightest Star.'

> "To be embraced, and to have my character embraced, and to have so many people tell me, 'Saru is my favorite character on the show,' it's wonderful."

05

"We got to go back and look at that, and find out what our relationship is with that predator species, and you saw that it's not quite like cattle. It's almost a religious, ritualistic thing that happens when it's time for certain members of the Kelpien society to be culled, and taken away for their death. It really is slaughter, but it's played and it's sold to us Kelpiens as our fulfilling of the great balance, whatever that means. It's our place, our duty, almost, and we can take pride that we're doing something very good for the balance

05 Farming, Kaminar-style, in "The Brightest Star."

06 Reunited with sister Siranna (Hannah Spear), in "The Sound of Thunder."

07 Burnham meets Siranna.

08 Saru takes a sip, in "The Sound of Thunder."

> "When Saru left Kaminar and left his world behind, it was like when I moved out of Indiana to seek my fame and fortune in Hollywood."

of nature on our planet of Kaminar.

"It brought up the question: is it really, or are we being sold a lie?" Jones muses. "Is that a great way to make dinner for the predator species, and they're selling it to us like, 'Just go along with us and don't fight us because it's best for all of us?' Or is there a better way?

"Saru is the one Kelpien who looks out to the sky, looks at his surroundings and thinks, 'There's got to be more out there. Is that all there is, what I'm experiencing here? Do we just survive the day until our death? Is that all we're here for?' I think that fulfills all our curiosities as people. We all look at where we grow up and our family situation and think, 'What's out there for me? What's the purpose of life? Is there more than what I'm experiencing right now?'"

FIRST CONTACT

Jones can't overemphasize the importance to him of the fine details revealed in "The Brightest Star." By depicting Saru's past, it shows how far he's come, from living in a primitive village, with its simple

lifestyle, to serving as first officer aboard a starship. In the episode, the young Kelpien tinkers with a high-tech device belonging to his species' predators, the Ba'ul, utilizing it to send a signal out into the galaxy. That signal soon brings him together for the first time with a figure who will loom large in his life: Philippa Georgiou, at this point a lieutenant.

"I have a young brother-in-law who, when he was nine years old, was taking apart radios and putting them together again," Jones recalls. "Self-taught. Now, he's one of the most-brilliant computer geniuses I've ever known. He never went to school for any of it. That's very much Saru. Saru took apart things he found and put them back together, and he found out a way to repurpose them into something new, to make contact with the outside world. That really was important to me to know that, okay, he had some innate smarts that he developed on his own.

"Now, you see that he made contact with the benevolent and kind and nurturing Lieutenant Georgiou, before she'd become Captain

Georgiou, and how he was taken into Starfleet. That's why Captain Georgiou had such a mother effect on him and held such a revered position in his life. And why he was so loyal to her."

Listen closely to the dialogue and music in "The Brightest Star," and you'll no doubt catch the swelling snippet of Alexander Courage's original series score, used by *Discovery* composer Jeff Russo to amplify the moment in which Saru decides to join Georgiou and leave his home planet. Viewers have loved it, and so did Jones.

"It was a beautiful bit," the actor says. "That scene takes me back to the 1960s and watching *Star Trek* for the first time. As a kid, living in Indianapolis, Indiana, you watch a show like that, that shows people in outer space exploring new worlds, and it makes you think, 'What's outside the border of Indiana for me?' So, I very much related to it. When Saru left Kaminar and left his world behind, it was like when I moved out of Indiana to seek my fame and fortune in Hollywood. It was also kind of boldly going into a world of the unknown, and that *Star Trek* theme

has helped inspire me all along the way. It was perfect in that moment for Saru."

BOLDLY GOING

That brings us to Season 2. Jones chooses his words carefully as he discusses *Discovery*'s sophomore season, lest he spoil anything for those who've yet to see it. He acknowledges that the war with the Klingons is over and, as a result, "We're back to exploring again, which will bring some nostalgia to those *Trek* purists who love the old *Trek*, and the boldly going, and the exploration, and the 'What's out there?'

09

INTERVIEW WITH THE VAMPYRE

One of Doug Jones' dream projects is finally coming to fruition. Years in the making, *Nosferatu*, with Jones in the title role, should arrive in theaters in 2019. Directed by David Lee Fisher, the film also features Emrhys Cooper, Joely Fisher, Jack Turner, and Jones's *Falling Skies* co-star, Sarah Carter.

"Of all the rubber bits I've played and worn over the years, the one thing left on my bucket list was to play a classic vampire, and, hopefully, Count Orlok in *Nosferatu*," Jones explains. "So, this is a dream come true for me.

"What's super exciting about it is that I actually got to play Count Orlok in the world that Max Schreck [the iconic Orlok of the 1922 *Nosferatu*] played it in, because every shot, every frame of our film, has a green screen element to it. That green screen element is filled in with footage and backdrop from the original film. So, I did actually get to play in the original movie, in a sense."

09 Saru and Siranna in simpler times, in "The Brightest Star."

"You'll see more of a peaceful dynamic among the crew," he elaborates. "We had some turmoil on board last year, especially for me personally, with the dynamic between Michael Burnham and Saru. Our brother/sister relationship was really competitive last year, and once we lost our mother figure, Captain Georgiou, I didn't let her off the hook for that for quite some time. So now, in Season 2, you'll see us bond, and have each other's back way more than before. And it's really quite heartwarming to watch. I hope that will really resonate with the fans."

And what else does he think fans will respond to?

"Well, let's see," he teases. "We Kelpiens, or me as a Kelpien, I learn a lot about my home planet. We visit my home planet in Season 2, and I learn some things that challenge what I know of as being a Kelpien and what it means to be a Kelpien. There's so much that comes into question now

> "We're back to exploring again, which will bring some nostalgia to those *Trek* purists who love the old *Trek*, and the boldly going, and the exploration."

that it rocks my world a little bit. So, we're going to get through that and also maybe deal with a predator species on my planet. I'm prey. So, who are the predators? The lingering question. We're going to find out who they are and what they're all about, and that relationship will unfold a bit."

Jones laughs when, as the conversation ends, he is asked about a very different predator figure: Mirror Georgiou, now an operative for Section 31. Surely Saru's threat ganglia must go into overdrive every time she's around?

"Oh, because she wants to eat my kind in the Mirror world?" Jones jokes. "Well, we never do warm up all the way to each other, I don't think. There's a built-in tension. As the season progresses, she's a part of Section 31 now and we have to trust her some, even though she keeps proving herself to be a bit of a loose cannon. So, Saru keeps her at a safe distance, but he has to trust her to some degree..." ✦

STAR TREK
DISCOVERY

PLAYING PIKE

For Anson Mount, portraying Captain Christopher Pike on *Star Trek: Discovery* represents a challenge not just in terms of joining the show in its second season, but in stepping into the shoes of not one but two actors who have previously portrayed Pike (and that's not counting the *Kelvin* Timeline one). Given all that, what does it take to play the *U.S.S. Enterprise*'s – and now the *U.S.S. Discovery*'s – captain?

Words: Ian Spelling

153

03

In a different universe – maybe even a mirror universe – Anson Mount might have played Gabriel Lorca, the devious fellow whose Machiavellian machinations drove much of the intrigue and drama during Season 1 of *Star Trek: Discovery*. It could have happened in the real world, too, truth be told – and it very nearly did. Of course, Jason Isaacs landed the role and made it his own, while Mount obviously impressed the powers that be at *Discovery*, as he went on to be cast in the pivotal part of Captain Christopher Pike for the show's second season.

"I auditioned," Mount says, explaining how Pike ultimately came his way. "I had auditioned…

I was close to getting Lorca, actually. I've got to say, they hired the right guy. I'm a big Jason Isaacs fan. I was a fan of Jason Isaacs before he did that role. I actually just watched *The Death of Stalin* on a plane. He's fantastic.

"But, with Pike, I think we'd had a good time meeting and talking and everything [about Lorca]. When this role came around, [the producers] were like, 'Hey, is Anson available?' My team said, 'Yeah.' They said, 'Will he audition?' I was like, 'Of course, I'll audition.' I don't want to be miscast in something. It felt good to them, it felt good to me, and we decided to do it. I've got to say, I was very excited to get the role, and then it was surreal for a while. It's still surreal."

02

"The thing that we all knew from the beginning – the only thing we really knew – is that Pike needed to be everything that Lorca was not."

01 Leading from the front in Season 2.

02 Anson Mount on stage with Michelle Yeoh and Shazad Latif at New York Comic-Con.

03 The captain in his chair.

Pike to *Discovery*

Mount arrives at *Discovery* with more than two decades of film and television work to his name. The actor, who hails from Illinois, was raised in Tennessee, and graduated from New York City's Columbia University with a degree in theater. He made his TV debut on *Ally McBeal* and has since added to his résumé everything from *Crossroads*, *Smallville*, *All the Boys Love Mandy Lane*, and *Lost* to *Dollhouse*, *Straw Dogs*, *Non-Stop*, *Hell on Wheels* (with *Star Trek: Deep Space Nine*'s Colm Meaney), and *Inhumans*.

Captain Pike remains one of *Star Trek*'s most interesting, even enigmatic, figures. Audiences,

in many ways, think they've seen more of him than they really have. The late Jeffrey Hunter portrayed Pike in the original *Star Trek* pilot, "The Cage," but elected not to return when NBC commissioned series creator Gene Roddenberry to produce a second pilot. Rather than let that entire first pilot go to waste, Roddenberry used footage from it for "The Menagerie" two-parter, adding a tremendously disfigured, wheelchair-bound Pike – now played by Sean Kenney – to the proceedings. More recently, Bruce Greenwood stepped into the role, serving as James T. Kirk's doomed mentor in *Star Trek (2009)* and *Star Trek Into Darkness*.

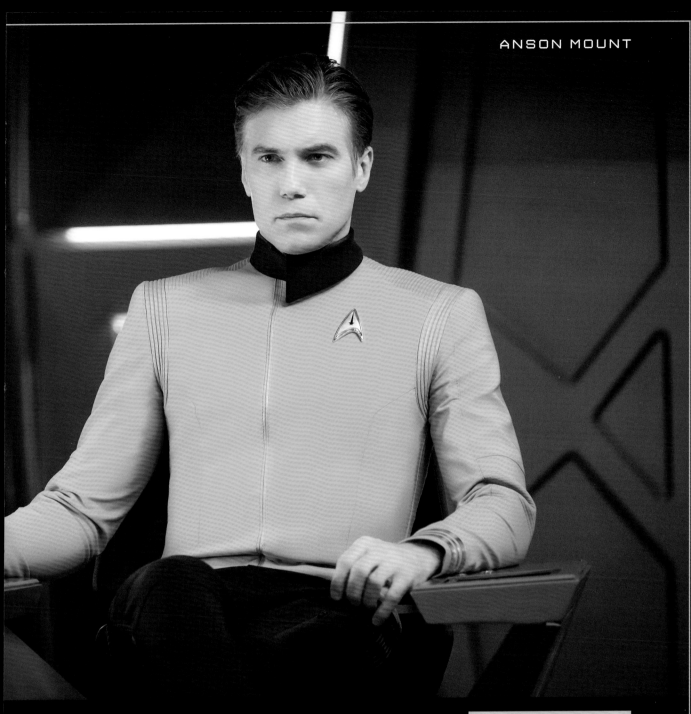

Planting Seeds

Discovery slyly planted the seeds for Pike's arrival during its first season. In "Choose Your Pain," Pike's name came up – along with April, Archer, Decker, and Georgiou – when Saru queried the computer about Starfleet's most-decorated captains. And, lastly, in the season finale "Will You Take My Hand?", the episode-ending hail – a priority-one distress call from an approaching Federation ship – was revealed to be from Captain Pike of the *U.S.S. Enterprise*.

All of that history, Mount notes, provided him with hints as to how to play Pike, as well as a certain degree of freedom in interpreting the character. "[He's] not like a blank page," the actor says. "There's a lot to go on in terms of the first script and my conversations with the writers, and what source material there was. And I knew that they wanted somebody the very opposite of Lorca. So, there were a lot of clues there.

"Having operated as a lead in a television show before [in the acclaimed *Hell on Wheels*], when you go to acting school, the one thing that they don't teach you is that one day, you're going to be on set and everybody's going to turn to look at you, and you've got to have answers. I kind of was

ORIGINAL FAN

Anson Mount didn't step on to either the *Enterprise* bridge or *Discovery* bridge for *Star Trek: Discovery* as a total newbie. He grew up watching the original series in syndication. "I've seen every episode multiple times," Mount says. "Then, *The Next Generation* started when I was in high school. After about the third season is when I went to college, and that's when I went into a lockbox for the next eight years."

SHORE LEAVE

Anson Mount's participation in *Star Trek: Discovery*, not surprisingly, has amplified the interest of *Star Trek* fans in his other current projects, of which there are two. He happily obliges a request to talk a bit about his podcast, *The Well* (at www.thewellpod. com), and the upcoming film *Midnight Climax*, a drama in which he co-stars with Jaime Ray Newman and Jason Patric.

"I am the co-host of *The Well* with my friend, Branan Edgens, who's a filmmaker and comes from an effects make-up background," he says. "The elevator pitch is that it's kind of like *Radiolab*, but instead of stories about science, it's stories about creative thinking. We come at it from all different angles, from not just artists, but we have a biologist, a football coach… We've got astrophysicists. Doug Jones is going to do an interview with us. People should check it out."

As for *Midnight Climax*, IMDB describes it as a drama "set during the true and unconscionable Central Intelligence Agency MK ULTRA drug experimentations in the early 1960s." Mount stars as Ford Strauss, the central character, who "is recruited to run a subsect of the program in a rural Mississippi Mental Hospital." Shedding a bit more light on the film, he explains: "That is with a first time writer-director who also comes from a military intelligence background. This guy, Joseph Sorrentino, I think he's got it. They're still finishing up the movie in post-production now. I play a northern behavioral psychiatrist working in Mississippi in the 1960s."

04

thrown into the deep end of the pool of leadership in that job. And that helped me to formulate this character, I'd say."

Researching the Future

As part of his research while prepping first to audition for Pike and then to play him, Mount checked out his predecessors' performances in the role. "I'd seen Bruce's [version of Pike] in the theater a while back, and then I had not seen 'The Cage' until I got this role," he recalls. "I just wanted to see the background. I didn't particularly think I resembled Jeffrey Hunter, at first, and then I happened to come across a picture of him playing Jesus [in the film *King of Kings*], and for a second I thought I had come across a picture of Cullen Bohannon [Mount's character in *Hell on Wheels*]. That's when I went, 'Oh, okay. All right.

Yeah, yeah, yeah. Okay, I guess there is a resemblance.'

"It's funny; I steal a lot as an actor, but I didn't really want to steal anything from any of these guys. For some reason, I felt like I needed to be respectful of what was there, but make it my own."

Worlds – and Pikes – soon collided. Mount met Hunter's son, Christopher, at 2018's San Diego Comic-Con, and he and Sean Kenney sat down for a lively chat and posed for a few photos when they both attended the official *Star Trek Las Vegas 2018* event. "Meeting Jeffrey Hunter's son, Chris, was incredible," Mount says enthusiastically. "He traveled all that way to Comic-Con just to tell me he thought his father would be happy with me being cast." As for Kenney, Mount states: "What a lovely guy. Sean is such an old-school Hollywood guy."

The Joy of Pike

Mount points out one of the joys of playing Pike: it's always fun to portray somebody you like. However, he hastens to add, he's "not particular," because, as an artist, it's ultimately his job to make every character – good, bad, or somewhere in between – effective and believable within the story being told. Still, breathing life into an honorable character such as Pike is "a great side benefit when it happens," he says.

"I'm not so concerned with characters being likeable, so much as understandable. I hope that Pike is both. The thing that we all knew from the beginning – the only thing we really knew – is that he needed to be everything that Lorca was not. I think that there's enough track laid for the character that that's backed up by the mythos. That's already in place.

elegant, and vivacious people I've ever met in my life. She really brings a tremendous amount of energy, work ethic, and respect to the set. When you see your number one working that hard – and when I say number one, I don't mean Number One in the *Star Trek* sense, I mean number one on the call sheet… When you see your number one working that hard and never complaining, you can't, either. She leads by example."

A Man for All Season?

It's anyone's guess – and fans are already speculating – how long Mount will be on the show. It could be a few episodes. Like with Isaacs, he could stick around for a season. Or, the actor could traverse the Final Frontier with *Discovery* indefinitely. How ready is Mount for a possibly lengthy run?

"I guess I've gotten to the point in my life and my career where I don't really think about those things," he replies candidly. "I've worked very hard. My twenties were a nightmare of worry and my thirties were a period of training myself to be present. My forties have been an enjoyable experience of being able to be in the present and not have to muscle myself into the present. I just sort of got used to doing it and not… I guess at a certain point you realize, 'Oh, wait, we live in a country that doesn't have a debtors' prison, and I'm not going to starve to death. Everything's going to work out.' I don't really think about that too much." ✦

04 Burnham and Pike with Section 31's Georgiou.

05 Anson Mount at *Star Trek Las Vegas*.

> "We're learning about Pike as we go. We've been feeling it out, redirecting, recalibrating here and there to see what feels right."

"And I'm learning about him as I go," Mount continues. "We're learning about him as we go. We've been feeling it out, redirecting, recalibrating here and there to see what feels right. It's great to be on a show that can afford to do that, to take the time to really develop a role the right way. It's not always like that. When you establish a character on TV, you tend to be careful about choices that you make because you're making them for a long period of time. You start with very general things. I know he probably had good parents, and he definitely had good mentors. And he knows that his greatest resource as a captain is his crew."

New Guy on the Set

It can be treacherous to be the new kid on an established series. Mount beamed aboard *Discovery* long after the show's regulars had bonded as a result of the long hours shooting Season 1 in Toronto, spending time together socially on weekends, and attending press and promotional events as a full-on team in the United States and abroad. Fortunately, Mount notes, the cast quickly embraced him.

"They've just made me feel welcome from day one," the actor says. "It starts from the top down. Sonequa Martin-Green is one of the most hospitable, loving, warm,

05

01

Pike's Plight
A Captain with Character

Prior to his starring role in *Star Trek: Discovery* Season 2, Captain Christopher Pike made just two Prime Timeline *Trek* appearances: in original pilot "The Cage," and in the original series first season two-parter "The Menagerie." So what can we glean from these glimpses about the second man to captain the *U.S.S. Enterprise*?

Words: Jay Stobie

Captain Christopher Pike's journey reveals itself in a nonlinear fashion, weaving back and forth between the years 2267 and 2254 in the *Star Trek* two-parter "The Menagerie" and the unaired pilot "The Cage," until finally looping around to the dawn of a new mission with the *U.S.S. Discovery* circa 2257. Despite his narrative's unique presentation, Pike's character displays a natural growth from one era to the next when examined chronologically. These elements, including the Starfleet officer's outlook on life, his connection with Spock, and his heroic deeds, combine to foster a greater understanding about the legendary captain.

Weight of Responsibility

When we first encounter Pike in 2254, the man's spirit and resolve face significant challenges following a disastrous mission on Rigel VII that resulted in numerous casualties, including the deaths of his yeoman and two other crew members.

Guilt and weariness tug at the captain as he considers resigning during a conversation with Doctor Boyce. Weighed down by responsibility, Pike envisions a more tranquil existence in a peaceful town and the pleasurable lifestyle enjoyed by proprietors on Regulus and the Orion colony. Boyce, who seems to know his commanding officer quite well, offers the somewhat prophetic advice, "A man either lives life as it happens to him,

meets it head-on and licks it, or he turns his back on it and starts to wither away."

Fortunately for Pike, the *U.S.S. Enterprise*'s detour to Talos IV interrupts his self-doubt and puts his place in the universe into perspective. When the captain is trapped in the Talosian zoo, his captors allow him to experience his scenic picnic and unburdened Orion fantasies alongside Vina. Yet rather than please Pike, these illusory scenarios cause him to understand Boyce's words and desire a path grounded in reality. The captain views the visions as deceptive, and opines, "You either live life, bruises, skinned knees, and all, or you turn your back on it and start dying."

Rejuvenation and Paralysis

Pike rejects the seductive offerings and tenaciously fights to return to his ship. Resolving the Talosian situation rejuvenates him, and endows him with an appreciation for his command. In the early episodes of *Star Trek: Discovery*'s second season, there are signs that Pike's fresh attitude continues into 2257 and beyond. Whether it's his enthusiastic handshake with Saru or his sly smirk in the captain's chair, Pike behaves as someone holding a new lease on life. He attempts to spread that energy to Burnham and the *Discovery* crew when he quips, "Wherever our mission takes us, we'll try to have a little fun along the way."

> "I'm tired of deciding which mission is too risky and which isn't. And who's going on the landing party and who doesn't. And who lives. And who dies."
>
> **CHRISTOPER PIKE**

Pike maintains his physical stature as late as a few months before Captain Kirk and the *Enterprise* visit Starbase 11 in 2267. Referring to Pike's condition before a training accident left him disabled, Commodore Mendez describes the man as "vital, active." Captain Pike continues to exhibit strong ties to the real world even after his injury, as, utilizing the beacon on his wheelchair, he voices his displeasure with Spock's plan to take him back to Talos IV.

Pike only acquiesces to spending his days in an imaginary world with his body intact after reliving 2254's events during Spock's trial, and realizing that reuniting with Vina and the Talosians will permit him to thrive without his corporeal limitations. Pike's mental rebound after the Rigel VII tragedy and preference for the truth unify his arc from "The Cage" to the final moments of "The Menagerie, Part II," when circumstances finally convince him to choose a falsified yet invigorating lifestyle over one filled with confinement and sadness.

02

The *Kelvin* Pike

The *Kelvin* Timeline's Christopher Pike respects Spock as well, as Bruce Greenwood's character relies on the Vulcan to handle first officer duties for the recently commissioned *U.S.S. Enterprise* in *Star Trek* (2009), and become acting captain when Nero imprisons Pike aboard the Romulan starship *Narada*. Spock vouches for Cadet James T. Kirk's theory about a trap at Vulcan and Nyota Uhura's translation skills, prompting Pike to take the threat seriously and go to red alert prior to dropping to impulse. However, Pike fosters an additional mentor-like relationship with Kirk, going so far as to appoint him as his first officer when the captain's chair reverts back to Pike in *Star Trek Into Darkness*.

Pike's fearlessness materializes in the alternate timeline, from voluntarily facing certain death by visiting Nero on the *Narada*, to his refusal to reveal the frequencies for Earth's defenses. Admiral Pike battles against the injuries he sustains on the Romulan ship, stepping out of his wheelchair and walking with a cane by the time Kirk loses his command.

Interestingly, while viewers never see the *Kelvin* Timeline's Pike deal with fantasies on Talos IV, Spock does describe experiencing emotions, such as confusion and loneliness, when he melds with Pike during his final moments. Those vulnerabilities harken back to the same doubts Prime Pike expresses to Doctor Boyce in "The Cage."

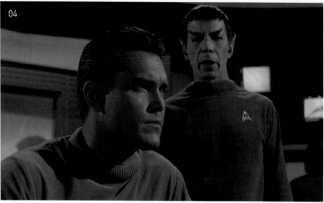

Pike and Spock

Spock serves as another tie that connects Pike's adventures over the years. As the *Enterprise*'s science officer in 2254, Spock transports to Talos IV with Pike's away team and later participates in his captain's rescue.

The pair clearly trust each other in a professional capacity. Pike relies on Spock as an integral part of his command crew, selecting the Vulcan to accompany him on the landing party. Spock works under Number One's leadership to devise a means to reacquire the captain.

However, no outward signs indicate a close personal relationship between Pike and Spock. The expedition to the Talos star system marks an early point in their friendship, with both men getting to know one another.

When Pike assumes command of *Discovery* in 2257, his dynamic with Spock has understandably evolved.

01 Pike and Number One with a captive Talosian.

02 Bruce Greenwood as the *Kelvin* Timeline Pike.

03 Pike in the *Enterprise* captain's chair.

04 Pike with Spock...

05 ...and with Doctor Boyce.

"I'm tired of deciding which mission is too risky and which isn't. And who's going on the landing party and who doesn't. And who lives. And who dies."

CHRISTOPER PIKE

Pike tells Michael Burnham that they share someone in common, referencing Spock and implying a more familiar demeanor for the captain and science officer. Pike also describes Spock's leave, believing that the Vulcan uncovered a question for which he sought out an answer. While at this stage we don't

know where *Discovery*'s second season will take us, it is nevertheless apparent that Pike and Spock's relationship has advanced significantly in the time since the mission on Talos IV.

An 11-year tour cements their personal bond of loyalty and friendship by 2267, when Spock willingly risks his career, his life, and the trust he shares with Kirk, McCoy, and the *Enterprise* crew to ferry Pike to the forbidden Talos star system.

In typical Spock fashion, the Vulcan permits his actions to reflect his feelings rather than expressing them vocally. Pike's reluctance to go to Talos IV, motivated in part by his desire for reality, may also be influenced by his awareness that Spock will be severely punished for the unauthorized mission. In fact, Pike only signals his desire to live with Vina and the Talosians *after* Uhura reports that Commodore Mendez does not intend to pursue

charges against Spock in this instance. Fittingly, Kirk requests that Spock escort Pike to the transporter room so that the wounded captain can begin his life anew.

Dedication to Duty

Captain Pike's heroism and dedication to duty function as additional elements that thread themselves throughout his career. After relating his doubts to Doctor Boyce, Pike still jumps back into his commanding persona when a report comes in about survivors inhabiting Talos IV's surface. Pike's awareness that the Rigel VII situation with Vina is fictitious does not prevent him from valiantly protecting Vina and defeating his opponent. As Vina describes the infinite possibilities the Talosians could provide with their mental prowess, Pike remains unfazed, and presses her for more information about the Talosians' motivations, capabilities, history, and methods. These questions help the captain ascertain the perplexing aliens' limited powers and lead to his eventual escape. Pike refuses to stay on the planet, as he prefers his reality, possibly due to his devotion to his crew, the Federation, and his mission.

By 2256, Starfleet has acknowledged Pike's audacity, as *Discovery*'s computer lists him among the most decorated captains in the episode "Choose Your Pain." It seems that commitment persists into 2257. Pike accepts a potentially dangerous assignment aboard *Discovery* with fervor, aware that bewildering challenges and perilous circumstances lurk ahead.

06 Pike with Number One, alias Majel Barrett.

07 Rare publicity photo for "The Cage," showing Pike with a fellow zoo specimen.

08 Sean Kenney as Pike in "The Menagerie."

Pike offers his vision concerning duty to his colleagues, elucidating his expectations for them with the words, "Starfleet is a promise… I give my life for you, you give your life for me… and nobody gets left behind." During one crisis, Pike proclaims, "If there's anybody down there, I'm not leaving them to die!" The captain's disposition indicates his continuing reliance on Federation values.

Courage and Sacrifice

Even as a fleet captain, Pike vaults into peril to save as many cadets as possible during a training accident that occurs months before Kirk arrives at Starbase 11 in 2267. Pike's sacrifice leaves his functioning mind trapped within a crippled body and prompts Spock to develop a strategy to unburden his former commander. Pike's hesitation pertaining to Spock's mutinous tactics demonstrates additional bravery, as he views imprisonment in his wheelchair as a better option than recognizing that Spock faces execution for traveling to Talos IV.

Pike's courage and devotion endure into the 24th Century, where the Christopher Pike Medal of Valor reigns as a significant accolade for the most exemplary Starfleet officers. Admiral Ross awards Captain Benjamin Sisko the decoration for his role in retaking Deep Space 9 during

Operation Return and his noteworthy participation in other Dominion War engagements. Ross specifically states that the medal is for "remarkable leadership and meritorious conduct against the enemy, and in particular for personal acts of bravery." Such language chronicles Pike's own exploits to perfection.

Whether portrayed by Jeffrey Hunter in 2254, Anson Mount in 2257, or Sean Kenney in 2267, Captain Christopher Pike remains a revered figure in the Federation long after he begins living on Talos IV. Pike's outlook on life, his relationship with Spock, and the boldness he conveys when in harm's way define his character, with each facet existing as a constant in his personal voyage while simultaneously progressing as the years pass. The traits paint a consistent picture that points to Pike as a man who heeds Boyce's advice and cherishes every second.

Much more will be learned about Captain Pike's fascinating legacy in *Star Trek: Discovery*'s second season, yet one thing is known for sure: we cannot wait to see what will transpire.

08

"The beard is a physical
embodiment of his
dishevelment, and
it's going to make my
shaved version of Spock
all the more exciting
and impressive when
it's revealed."

STAR TREK
DISCOVERY
I AM SPOCK

Of all the characters introduced to *Star Trek: Discovery*'s second season, Spock is by far the most iconic. The Vulcan has been an intrinsic part of *Star Trek* since its earliest days, for many symbolizing the very essence of the show. All of which makes portraying him a daunting task for newcomer Ethan Peck, who in a face-to-face interview with *Star Trek Magazine* reveals how he's been studying Leonard Nimoy's performances and writings in order to become his own version of Spock.

Words: Mark Newbold

Star Trek Magazine: How does it feel to be joining this amazing *Star Trek* family for Season 2 of *Star Trek: Discovery*?
Ethan Peck: I'm so overjoyed; it's such an incredible honor, and it's taken some time to really begin to feel like I'm a part of it because it's such a daunting role and task. I wasn't sure if I'd be able to do it, and everybody's just made me feel worthy – there's such great support on set. Everybody's so wonderful, as I'm sure you've seen. It's like a dream come true, it's very surreal.

What's been the biggest surprise of the process so far?
There are a few. Probably discovering – no pun intended – that the role I was reading for was Spock. I didn't know what it was for in the very beginning *(laughs)*, and when I found that out I was just like, "Oh my gosh, I'm glad I didn't know this earlier!" Because a gift of that is that the very first set of audition sides was very much my own, so the seed of this Spock

feels very personal. Obviously, once I had that information, there was a lot more knowledge to be gained about the Spock he will become, portrayed so beautifully and wonderfully by Nimoy in the original series.

Because you didn't realize you were auditioning for Spock, do you feel like you have some ownership of the process of creating this iteration of him?
Yeah, absolutely, it definitely feels my own in a lot of ways, but obviously it's all done with great respect and reverence for what they did in the '60s. That's the benchmark and that's the light at the end of the tunnel, because my Spock begins in a place that you may not immediately recognize him. We had to start him someplace to take him to readiness for Kirk and for *Enterprise*.

What was the character description that was given to you when you were auditioning for the role?
(Laughs) Originally, he was Andorian. I could tell that

ETHAN PECK ON
FANDOM

Star Trek Magazine: Have you had much feedback yet from the fans, and are they welcoming you so far?

Ethan Peck: I've stayed away from looking at any press about it, or reactions. As I said before, I really want to be liked, and that's not useful to me in my creative process. If I just have my immediate experience of me as this character on set... Everybody's so warm and positive and I really want to maintain that energy.

People aren't going to like me, and I accept that; that's okay, people are entitled to their opinions. If everybody liked me that wouldn't make sense, there'd be something wrong. I really try to stay away from the press; I don't want to be influenced by it, because I think I'm on a really great journey right now.

02

03

it would appear to be somebody who was experiencing emotions for the first time, and was trying to intellectualize them, but that wasn't working, and the emotions were still erupting. I just never thought that it would be Spock. I was like, "Is it Data, I don't know."

This is Spock between "The Cage" and his posting years later on Kirk's *Enterprise*, so he's a slightly looser Spock. Is there more freedom for this Spock?

There is and there isn't. What makes Spock so special – as a character that teaches us about ourselves as humans – is that he's half Vulcan, half human. He's got this built-in epic conflict. We see him in a place where he's unraveled. I think that when you haven't experienced emotion, my own interpretation of it is that there's fighting, there's wrestling with it – sometimes logical, sometimes severely illogical, and sometimes emotional. That's done with all due respect to who he will become, and hopefully we do that right. It's a very delicate dance and balance.

You've mentioned Nimoy, but did you also look at Zachary Quinto's version in the *Kelvin* Timeline films?

Oh yeah, of course, I absolutely looked

at Quinto's version. I saw those movies in theaters; I love them, and I think he did an amazing job, but my benchmark is really Nimoy's Spock.

Did you go back and watch Nimoy's early performances?

I'm still working my way through it, because I had to catch up on Season 1 of *Discovery*. I met with the Nimoy family, which was incredible. They were so warm and curious. It was the first step of making me feel worthy of this, because they were just so lovely. I watched the documentaries they each made, *For The Love Of Spock* and *Remembering Leonard Nimoy*, about COPD [Chronic Obstructive Pulmonary Disease] and his struggle with that. They really inspired me to be curious, and that was really the best advice I could have gotten, because Spock is ultimately a curious being. He wants to understand.

I've been watching slowly because I really need to internalize what he did. I need to watch an episode and study what he's doing, and so I can't really blast through them. I also read *I Am Not Spock*, which he wrote in '75, and I'm amazed nobody told me to read that first because he talks about who Spock is to him and how Spock becomes a piece of him. I feel like I've

and I think that's happening. I hope that's happening.

You're playing an iconic character in a franchise that has a very intense fan base. Does that frighten you at all?
Oh yeah. It definitely frightens the heck out of me because I want him to be great. I'm a perfectionist myself, which can also be a flaw. I want to be liked, definitely, but at the same time that's not useful for my process. There's time that I spend with that thought and there's time to just focus and be inspired by the material I'm given and the research I've done and the experiences that I'm having.

When people think of Spock it's often a very one-dimensional view – he's the logic guy. As you go through this process, what are some of the things that you feel people misunderstand about Spock?
There's a great interaction between him and Kirk where Kirk says, "Spock, you'd make a great computer," and Spock says, "Thank you, Captain" [see "The Return of the Archons"] – because that is the Vulcan way, to be logical. Ultimately, I think he's got a great depth about him. In *Wrath of Khan*, Kirk says how he's one of the most human beings

spent so much time with him, he's like a voice in my head now.

Where is the relationship between Michael Burnham and Spock when we meet them in Season 2?
They haven't seen each other in a long time, and there's a reason for that.

Can you tell us a bit about the first time that you went onto the sets. Did you have a moment to yourself?
I came out for a prosthetics and make-up test about a month before I started, and one of the wonderful ADs asked if I wanted a tour. I said, "Yeah!" The sets were just masterpieces. The level of detail and craftsmanship all around, it's just unbelievable. It feels like another world, it was like being transported.

What did it feel like as an actor to be walking onto the bridge of the *U.S.S. Discovery*?
I was very intimidated, because what they do is such high-level work. I mean, Sonequa Martin-Green is so talented and she's also a mother. I don't know how she does it to be honest, because it's such a marathon. Everybody made me feel so welcome, and I admire them – they inspire me and I've grown because of them.

> "Burnham and Spock haven't seen each other in a long time, and there's a reason for that."

Do you think that Spock will become a part of you, like he did with Nimoy?
That's a very interesting question. Yeah, I do. I have this amazing opportunity to spend so much time with such an interesting character. If you do a guest spot on a television show it can be for a week or so. A film can be a month, but *Discovery* is many months, and that's one thing that Nimoy talks about in his book. He writes discussions between himself and Spock in his own mind. I've done my best to develop an inner Spock voice, and so there are times when I feel frightened on set or have some anxiety about some scene, and I try to talk to myself, like, "Your emotions are illogical, they will not serve you," that kind of thing. That's the thing that influenced me and kind of seeped beneath the surface.
I'm not trying to imitate what he's done, because that would be a fruitless exercise, but I've really tried to capture and internalize his spirit,

05

01 Ethan Peck as Spock, with Leonard Nimoy as Spock.

02 Peck on stage at New York Comic-Con.

03 Spock as he appears in "The Cage."

04 Spock at his station.

05 Zachary Quinto as Spock.

ETHAN PECK FILMOGRAPHY

06

07

06 *Star Trek II: The Wrath of Khan* – a touchstone for Peck in terms of Spock's emotional side.

07 Kirk and Spock in "The Return of the Archons," which for Peck provided an insight into Spock's logical side.

that [he's ever] known, and I think that's really who Spock is. He's got a great heart and great empathy, and room for emotion; but ultimately, I think his execution is logical.

Did you always know you were going to have the beard?
I didn't know I was going to have a beard. I was told before I went out there, "Don't shave." I was like, "Don't shave? Oh, okay." It's well thought out. It's a physical embodiment of his dishevelment, that we find him in.

You're wearing a Borg T-shirt, so you're obviously a *Star Trek* fan. Is that how you fell in love with *Trek*, through *Star Trek: First Contact*, or was it another movie or episode?
First Contact is my childhood *Trek* movie, so to get to work with [director and star] Jonathan Frakes was frikkin' amazing. I'd seen episodes here and there, but I watched that movie a lot when I was a kid, it's so great.

With Spock being part of that classic triumvirate with Kirk and McCoy, do you feel that your performance, as much as leaning toward "The Cage" version of the character, is building him toward those kinds of relationships?

I'm more focused on the spirit of Spock in the original series. What I mean by that is that you really see Nimoy with a great awareness for the emotional weather going on around him on the bridge, internalizing it, and then acting logically. Very rarely do you see him acting emotionally. In regard to the relationships, no, not so much, because that's so far in the future, about 10 years ahead. My attention is on the people around me – Captain Pike, Michael Burnham – really developing those relationships and finding Spock's place among them.

"My benchmark is really Nimoy's Spock."

Nimoy and Quinto both tap into the sarcasm that Spock has. He uses logic and he's a very serious character, but they both managed to capture his humor.
The writers are doing a really great job with that. I think it's a little more tongue in cheek in the original series. I think our show is very austere in a lot of ways: the stakes are really high and it's a very serious and fraught world. I'm playing less with self-awareness, but with the timing of it. There's some really great, biting lines. Sometimes you're laughing with Spock in the original series – you can see kind of a glimmer and a twinkle – whereas in this one you'll be laughing at me, I hope. Which is fun, because the stakes are super high.

What are you most excited to share with audiences during Season 2?
I'm excited for them to see – this ties in with what Kirk says in *Wrath of Khan* – I'm excited for fans to experience Spock's depth and his vulnerability. ⨍

As Paul Stamets and Hugh Culber, Anthony Rapp and
Wilson Cruz tugged at fans' heartstrings during Season
1 of *Star Trek: Discovery*, both in their portrayal of their
characters' relationship, and in how that relationship was
tragically, violently truncated. Or so it seemed back then...
because the events of Season 2 have opened a surprising
new chapter in the lives of this stellar couple.

WORDS: IAN SPELLING
ADDITIONAL REPORTING: MARK NEWBOLD

STAR-CROSSED LOVERS...?

01

02

Lieutenant Commander Paul Stamets and Doctor Hugh Culber belong together, but is it really meant to be? And if so, how?

Those are just two of the many questions that have been swirling around the couple as Season 2 of *Star Trek: Discovery* has unfolded. That's because in Episode 10 of Season 1, "Despite Yourself," Voq/Ash Tyler snapped Culber's neck – a sudden, brutal act of violence that changed everything for everyone. Complicating matters, Doctor Culber seemingly lived on in the mycelial network, perhaps as a man, maybe as more of an essence.

In our quest for answers, *Star Trek Magazine* sat down with the actors who portray Stamets and Culber, Anthony Rapp and Wilson Cruz, as filming on *Discovery* Season 2 wrapped, picking their brains over the course of a trio of conversations. Here's what the duo, longtime friends, had to say…

Star Trek Magazine: We know that Doctor Culber is back, but we're not sure how or for how long. So, how much of Stamets' pure grief over his partner's death will we see?
Anthony Rapp: I've been very satisfied with the time and space that's been given to talk about and deal with the aftermath.

Wilson Cruz: I'll say.
AR: It's really meaningful, and I think it's also very much in the spirit of where *Trek* has always been. You get to know the human beings inside of the starship. And, on a very personal level, any storytelling that deals with grief is very meaningful to me. It's something that's been a part of my life. I'm pretty picky about stories that deal with grief. So, I've been very satisfied with how it's been approached.
WC: I can also say that a lot of people were upset when Culber was killed off last season – spoiler alert! I think that once you get through the second season, you'll see that there's a reason why he had to die the way he did, ►

01 Love knows no bounds... except, seemingly, the divide between our world and the mycelial one. ("Saints of Imperfection")

02 Culber and Stamets in Season 1's "Choose Your Pain."

03 Tending to Tilly in "Saints of Imperfection."

04 Tilly, Culber, and Stamets in Season 1's "Si Vis Pacem, Para Bellum."

> "Any storytelling that deals with grief is very meaningful to me. It's something that's been a part of my life."
>
> ANTHONY RAPP

▶ when he did. This story will connect all of those dots, and where he ends up will be a good explanation as to why.

Wilson, when you first landed the role, did the producers tell you that Culber was going to die?
WC: No, they didn't tell me right away. They did tell me two episodes before, so I had a good month to process that and get all of my Puerto Rican anger out about it, which I'm glad no one got to see. Shortly thereafter, because I think they were still working out how it was going to happen, they let me know.

What's it like to portray a dead man?
WC: What can I say? It was really an opportunity for me to use my imagination and imagine what it would be like for me to deal with the consequences of being brutally murdered, and what that loss means. It was devastating to play. It was hard.
AR: I think it's done with a really unusual and interesting approach.

Anthony, what can you say about performing across from a man who's playing a dead man?

AR: Because of that – the mysteries of it, and the science of it, and the personal nature of it – it feels like it's been put into a really wonderful mixture that feels original, and human, and complicated, and rich.

WC: Like I said, there are consequences to what happened.

AR: It's not a magic wand thing. It's not a snap your fingers thing. It's not easy. It's hard work, which is what everything that's meaningful and matters should be.

Looking back to the start of Season 2, can we assume that Culber realizes he's dead?

WC: He is where we left him [at the end of Season 1], but even for him, so much of what he was doing right after the event was trying to get [Stamets'] attention, to alert him to what was going on in the mycelial network that he needed to be aware of in order to save the universes. Now, all of that is over, and he's left having to deal with where he's at and what that means for him.

AR: There's a scientific basis for the fantastical elements of how [Culber] is able to come back. In the physical universe, energy doesn't die. It transforms. And the nature of mycelia is that they recycle matter and energy. They are nature's recyclers. He's in a mycelia network. How did he wind up there? These questions get addressed and answered in a way that…

WC: *(Dramatically)* Which is why we find him where we left him.

AR: It's taken seriously. Yes, it is fantastical in a way, but it's also rooted in things that do connect up with some scientific [principles]…

WC: As so much of our show is.

> ## "We haven't seen a relationship like this. I've never had the opportunity to play one."
>
> WILSON CRUZ

When it comes to Stamets and Culber, it seems this isn't merely, "Oh, look, a gay couple. Isn't that nice?" The writers are striving to build up your characters, what your love story means.

WC: And I promise you, just based on what we've already done, that we've taken that to a whole other level this season. We haven't seen a relationship like this. I've never had the opportunity to play one. So, it's been really satisfying as an actor. I'm excited to get to a point where I can talk about it, because it's been so incredibly satisfying [to play], and nerve-wracking, because you want to get it right. ▶